FINDING YOUR WAY

after

Your Child Dies

FINDING YOUR WAY

after

Your Child Dies

Phyllis Vos Wezeman
Kenneth R. Wezeman

ave maria press **Notre Dame, Indiana**

International Standard Book Number: 0-87793-700-1

Cover and text design by Brian C. Conley

Printed and bound in the United States of America.

Library of Congress Cataloging-in-Publication Data
Wezeman, Phyllis Vos.
    Finding your way after your child dies / Phyllis Vos Wezeman, Kenneth
R. Wezeman.
        p. cm.
    ISBN 0-87793-700-1 (pbk.)
    1.Children--Death--Religious aspects--Christianity--Meditations. 2. Parents--Prayer-books and devotions--English. 3. Consolation. I. Wezeman, Kenneth R. II. Title.
    BV4907 .W49 2000
    248.8'66--dc21
                                                00-011328

In memory of Charles Douglas Jewell . . .

"Charlie"

May 24, 1987—March 4, 1999

who bore witness to the love of Jesus in both
his life and his death,

and

In appreciation of Chuck, Lisa, Kaitlyn,
and Brandon Jewell . . .

for sharing faith and friendship.

Contents

Introduction

An empty place at mealtime . . .
    an unoccupied room in the house . . .
        a vacant seat in the car . . .
            reminders of the loss of your child occur
            from day to day.

Classes at the church . . .
    popcorn at the movies . . .
        students on the bus . . .
            recurrences of your grief take place week
            after week.

Baby books . . .
    cemetery visits . . .
        family pictures . . .
            remembrances of your daughter or son
            surface from time to time.

Birthdays . . .
    holidays . . .
        seasons . . .
            reflections suggest the absence of your child
            year after year.

Driver's licenses . . .
    graduation parties . . .
        wedding celebrations . . .
            rituals recall the death of your child
            throughout a lifetime.

Finding Your Way After Your Child Dies is a book that offers parents who have experienced the death of a child an opportunity to deal with their loss—losses that occur daily, weekly, from time to time, once a year, and throughout a lifetime. This resource develops fifty-two themes—ranging from baptisms to birthdays, Christmas to church, and pets to possessions—to help fathers and mothers acknowledge a loss, express feelings associated with the change, and recognize the experience as an opportunity for grief, as well as for growth.

Each theme in *Finding Your Way After Your Child Dies* is developed through a consistent, easy-to-use format:

REFLECTION	provides an overview of the specific theme,
RITUAL	offers suggestions to explore the theme,
READING	includes a Scripture passage or verse for reflection on the theme,
RESPONSE	offers a prayer that summarizes the theme.

While these fifty-two meditations are intended for fathers and mothers who have experienced the death of a daughter or a son, they may be easily adapted for use in small and large group worship, education, outreach, and nurture settings. They are also appropriate for use by catechists, directors of religious education/formation, family members, grandparents, pastors, siblings, teachers, and youth directors/leaders.

Finding Your Way After Your Child Dies reminds parents—and others—to turn to God in every circumstance of life. Regardless of the situations that occur in a day—or in a lifetime—God is with us. God is always present to us and for us. God's word assures us that we can spend time with God, pour out our heart to God, and be assured of God's love—a love that survives any loss.

A PERSONAL WORD FROM THE AUTHORS

Some of you know the story of the Jesus Doll. Some of you don't. All of you should.

The Jesus Doll is a handcrafted work of art developed by liturgical artist Brenda Grauer of "In Stitches" in Chagrin Falls, Ohio. Brenda created the Jesus Doll to be a visual reminder of Christ's constant presence with children, youth, and adults. Although we were first introduced to the Jesus Doll many years ago, two women from our church purchased one at an ecumenical educators' event in Chicago in February 1999.

During the message on February 7, we introduced the doll to the children and offered them the privilege of carrying it for a Sunday. Here's how it works. The names of kindergartners through fifth graders are placed in a "box." Each week one is drawn from the container and posted on the bulletin boards. If the child is in his or her class by 9:30 a.m., the person has the opportunity to carry the doll for the rest of the morning—Sunday School, Celebration Service, and Second Hour. If the child is not in class at 9:30 a.m., the doll is delivered to the toddler or the pre-K room so younger children may enjoy it for the day.

About a month after we purchased the doll—Monday, March 1, to be exact—Phyllis prepared for a busy week which included three days in California to explore the possibility of beginning a parent education program in our congregation. During the day, she placed the Jesus Doll on top of her file cabinet, reached into the box, and pulled the slip for Sunday, March 7. As Phyllis wrote a fifth grader's name on the forms, she wondered how a "big kid" would react to carrying the doll. But, she concluded, if anybody could handle it, this eleven-year-old boy would be the one. He already "carried" Jesus with him in so many ways—by inviting friends to church, by helping busy teachers, and by sharing great smiles. Phyllis left for California.

Late Thursday night, March 4, Ken picked Phyllis up at the airport. On the way home he told her about an accident on the Indiana Toll Road that had occurred earlier in the day. It involved a semi-truck, a State Trooper's car, and a sports utility vehicle. Three people had been killed and three others were injured. Their names had not been released. We didn't think too much more about the tragedy until several phone calls came in the early hours of the morning. Charlie Fewell, a member of our church—along with his grandpa Doug Fites and a young officer—was killed in the accident. Shocked and saddened, Phyllis woke her family to tell them the news. As we read reports in the paper, listened to information on the radio, and watched coverage on TV, we remembered Charlie—and then, Phyllis remembered the Jesus Doll. The name of the eleven-year-old fifth grader she had pulled on Monday was Charlie's. Charlie Fewell had the privilege of carrying the Jesus Doll, her handwritten note read; instead, Charlie was now being carried by Jesus.

Later in the day, Phyllis shared the story with the senior pastor—who relayed it to the Fewells. "If they'd like the doll," she remarked, "they may have it." Late Friday night, Charlie's dad, Chuck, called us at home. "We'd like to have the Jesus Doll. Could you bring it to us tomorrow?" We made arrangements to meet Saturday afternoon.

In the meantime, we searched for ways to talk with the children of our church on Sunday morning. We pondered ways to discuss the death of their lively friend, Charlie. Perhaps the answer was the Jesus Doll! Phyllis called Brenda Grauer, the designer, and asked if she could ship a new Jesus Doll to us by Sunday morning. She would try.

On Sunday morning, we prayed for the words to use—and the strength to say them—when the children arrived. As the fifth graders—Charlie's class—gathered in the music room, we were waiting—with the "new" Jesus Doll. We spoke about the process of picking a name and offering someone the privilege of carrying the Jesus Doll for the day. We told them that the name Phyllis had picked for that morning was Charlie's. We talked about how much Charlie loved Jesus—and how much Jesus loved Charlie. Grade by grade, class by class, the process continued. The Jesus Doll was a tangible—and touchable—reminder of Jesus' closeness and care. Later in the day when we visited the funeral home, we noticed that the "first" Jesus Doll had been placed in the corner of Charlie's casket. And, just before the coffin was closed at church, the Jesus Doll was removed and carried into the sanctuary by Charlie's grandma—whose husband had also died in the crash. Grandma Nancy, as well as other family members, caringly clutched the Jesus Doll during the memorial service.

Why are we telling this story? First, because it has impacted our lives—and the lives of many children, youth, and adults in our congregation, community, and beyond. Every time we see the Jesus Doll it is a trigger that reminds us of Charlie's death—as well as Charlie's life. Most importantly, though, we share the story because the Jesus Doll is a constant reminder that everything we do as the family of faith is about carrying Jesus with us. Every moment of every day is about making faith-life connections, with Jesus as our focus.

As you use the Reflections, Rituals, Readings, and Responses in this book, it is our prayer that they may help you to draw nearer to Jesus and to remember Jesus' nearness to you.

Blessings,
Ken and Phyllis Wezeman

Allowance

What will you do with the allowance?

REFLECTION

Allowances are often part of a family ritual, given at a particular time of the week or month. In some households allowances may be passed out less formally when a child requests money to save or spend. Ideally, allowances are a learning tool for a child. As young people spend their allowances, they discover how to handle resources and to budget money. Many families suggest that a portion of an allowance be tithed or given to a charitable cause. Some boys and girls pick an organization to support with "their" money. The organization that is chosen may become quite important to that child, and to the entire family.

When a family loses a child the ritual of the allowance is disrupted. It is another moment when everyone is reminded of their loss. It can, however, also become a moment that honors the life of the loved one who died if a cause that was important to the child is remembered with a gift. It can be a way that the love that was expressed in life can continue to be experienced, even in the face of death.

RITUAL

- Continue to place the allowance in a bank and donate the money to an organization the child supported.

- Establish a memorial fund in honor of the child to benefit a charitable cause.

- Place the allowance money in the church offering each week.

- Pray for the needs of the organization that received the allowance money on a regular basis.

- Use a short ritual each time a gift of money is given—or received for a memorial fund—such as:

  Dear God, May this gift of money be used to bless and enrich the lives of *name of recipient* as *name of child* blessed and enriched our lives. We dedicate this gift to you and to *name of child*'s memory, in love. Amen.

READING

Each of you must give as you have made up your mind, not reluctantly or under compulsion, for God loves a cheerful giver (2 Corinthians 9:7).

RESPONSE

Lord, Thank you for *name* and for the difference he or she made in our life and in the lives of others. Amen.

Anniversary of Death

How will you face the anniversary of your child's death?

REFLECTION

Once every year those who have lost a loved one face the anniversary of the death. Great dread may mount as the day approaches—especially in the first few years. As one thinks about the day it may be mentally re-lived with all the emotions that accompanied it the first time. On the other hand, some people may avoid thinking about it. A few may even be able to let the day pass without experiencing any emotional pain.

Most of us, however, do think about the anniversary of the death of our child. It can be so painful that it may be hard to function at work or in school. We may even have to take time off. It may be disruptive to our families because everyone's nerves are on edge. It can also be a problem when one person finds the anniversary emotionally upsetting and another deals with the problem by blocking it out of consciousness as much as possible. When two people with such extreme coping methods live together, especially the child's father and mother, it may cause great conflict. The person who feels all the emotion may think that the other person is cold or callous, and the person who blocks out the pain may think that the one who feels the pain is being histrionic. In fact, both are hurting but have very different ways of experiencing their pain. There are other ways of expressing this grief as well. Some people may be irritable or angry, exploding about little things in bursts of rage.

There is no "correct" way to grieve or to remember the anniversary of the death of someone we love. It is important to give each other the "space" we need to mourn in our own way and to try to understand each other's needs.

RITUAL

- Acknowledge the anniversary of your child's death by including a notice in a church or school bulletin or newsletter. Take the opportunity to thank people for the support they have shown through the year(s).

- Design or purchase a piece of jewelry—earrings, necklace, pin, ring, or tie tack—that displays the birthstone of your child. Wear the item every day or only on the anniversary of your daughter's or son's birth and death.

- Give a floral arrangement or a plant to a church or school on the anniversary of your child's death. Visit the cemetery and place flowers on the grave. Plant a tree in a private or a public place in honor of the life of your loved one.

- Hold a family gathering on the anniversary of your child's death. Spend time with immediate and extended relatives, as well as close friends and important persons in your family of faith. Support each other emotionally, physically, and spiritually; share stories that are important to each person.

- Offer a special mass or prayer liturgy on the anniversary of your child's death. Include a moment of silence in memory of your loved one or have his or her name read publicly during the service.

READING

As God's chosen ones, holy and beloved, clothe yourselves with compassion, kindness, humility, meekness, and patience. Bear with one another and, if anyone has a complaint against another, forgive each other; just as the Lord has forgiven you, so you also must forgive. Above all, clothe yourselves with love, which binds everything together in perfect harmony (Colossians 3:12-14).

RESPONSE

Lord, not all anniversaries are happy occasions. Some are hard for us to face. Give us the grace to not insist that everyone must grieve the same way we do. Help us to be patient with each other. Amen.

Baby Books, Family Scrapbooks, Photo Albums

What memories do the pictures prompt?

REFLECTION

Baby books, family scrapbooks, and photo albums are the record of a household's history. Some of these items—in the form of compact discs, sixteen mm. movies, formal and informal photographs, thirty-five mm. slides, or video cassettes—may be stored in boxes, drawers, and envelopes. Regardless of their format, or their organization, they chronicle the life of children, youth, and adults. For the nuclear family these collections contain memories of many different kinds of events, from birth to old age. Adults and children alike love to look through these pages, papers, and programs, and recall special family moments and milestones. In addition, these resources often record information about previous generations and form a link to the family's past. Albums, collections, and scrapbooks are also treasures to pass on for the future. Possessions like these are so unique that they cannot be replaced. In the event of a natural disaster, like a tornado, or an unfortunate experience, such as a house fire, you simply cannot go to a store and buy a substitute.

When a family has lost a child these baby books, scrapbooks, and photo albums become even more important. If the child died at or shortly after birth, the photographs taken in the hospital may be the only tangible memories available to the parents. Many friends and relatives did not have the opportunity to see your child. It might even be difficult for them to comprehend the reality of your loss. Pictures may make your loss more real to them. In fact, they may help to make it more real to you, too. Often we might feel like the death of a newborn is something that didn't really happen. Pictures help us face our grief again when this occurs.

Although it can be emotionally stressful to look through picture albums and scrapbooks, in the long run we are glad to have them. They ultimately bring more joy than pain. In fact, we wish we had more. Other family members are also "a part of the picture" and have a need to remember their past. In fact, if one has children who are born after the death of a daughter or son, or who were very young when the loss occurred, those pictures may be their only link with part of their family.

RITUAL

- Display pictures of your child in a private or public place in your home. Create a photo collage to hang on a wall or exhibit favorite photos in special frames.

- Organize or re-organize photos—especially snapshots—that may be in boxes, closets, drawers, end tables, or envelopes. Chronicle the life of your daughter or son and add captions or comments.

- Reflect silently, verbally, or in writing—alone or with others—on the stories connected with each item in a baby book, piece in a family scrapbook, or picture in a photo album. Also select special times to look at these memories, such as on your child's birthday or during a holiday season like Christmas or Easter.

- Select a new format for favorite pictures. Transfer snapshots to CDs or slides to videos. Take photos to a copy center and have them printed on fabric to use as the basis of a quilt or a wall hanging. For safety reasons, consider keeping a CD or a video of favorite photos in a separate location, such as in a bank vault or at the home of a relative.

- Share extra photos with others, including family members, friends, and people in the pictures.

READING

He will feed his flock like a shepherd;

he will gather the lambs in his arms,

and carry them in his bosom,

and gently lead the mother sheep.

—Isaiah 40:11

RESPONSE

Thank you, God, for the precious links to our loved ones that we have in pictures. We thank you for the picture you have given us of yourself as the tender Shepherd of our children. Help us to carry that picture always in our minds. Amen.

Baptism

What are your baptism memories?

REFLECTION

A baptism is a very special and joyful event. Through the sacrament of baptism, a child—or an adult—becomes part of the family of God. Baptism is a holy, visible sign and seal, appointed by God, of the washing away of sins and the promise of eternal life. It is a happy time for parents both because of the spiritual significance of the occasion and because of the joy that accompanies a new addition to the family. A baptism usually brings together friends, relatives—even the whole extended family of the congregation—to celebrate the event.

To the parent who is grieving the loss of a child, a baptism may produce mixed emotions. On the one hand, you may be happy for the family member, fellow parishioner, or friend who is presenting a child for baptism. On the other hand, you may be reminded of your own loss and your own empty arms. If your child was stillborn you may feel extremely envious. The joy of other parents may simply highlight your own grief.

We may remember our child's baptism with joy as well as with sadness. Most of us take comfort in the knowledge that our child was baptized. He or she was a part of God's family. There may be additional complications, for example if circumstances did not allow for your child to be baptized. There may not have been time to perform your child's baptism at birth or you may not have been a Christian at the time your child died. In such instances you may have profound regret that adds to your grief. Baptized or not, we may remember that our Lord was the one who said, "Let the little children come to me."

RITUAL

- Find a scallop shell—large or small—and set it in a private or a public place in your home as a symbol of baptism. Consider placing a picture taken at your child's baptism into a frame decorated with shells.

- Gather items related to your child's baptism—articles of clothing, a baptismal certificate, or cards and notes—in a memory box or store them in a special place.

- Light your child's baptismal candle each year on the anniversary date of your child's baptism.

- Send a card or note, or offer a prayer or a word of encouragement, to parents presenting a child for baptism in your parish.

- Suggest that your parish start a tradition of presenting a baptismal banner, stole, or towel—including the name of the child, his or her date of birth, and the date of the sacrament—to each family after a baptismal service.

READING

Then little children were being brought to him in order that he might lay his hands on them and pray. The disciples spoke sternly to those who brought them; but Jesus said, "Let the little children come to me, and do not stop them; for it is to such as these that the kingdom of heaven belongs" (Matthew 19:13-14).

RESPONSE

Thank you, Lord, for welcoming our children as your own. We find comfort in your warmth and care for little ones. We entrust our child, *name*, to you, confident of your great love. Amen.

Birthday of Child

How will you celebrate a birthday?

REFLECTION

In most cultures birthdays are a time for celebration. For older people they may be a celebration of past growth or accomplishment. For younger people birthdays are more likely to be an anticipation of new and greater things to come. For those who have lost a child the birthday can be a time of profound sadness because there are no new and greater things in the future. For the beloved child, the future will never come. This realization is especially painful the first few years that the child's birthday is remembered. It is natural to dwell on the loss, not only of our child, but also of the future.

In contrast to the pain of loss, there can also be a joy in remembering a birthday. One may recall many aspects of the life of the child. Past birthday celebrations may have especially happy memories associated with them. Although, for some, the joy of birthday memories may be present the first year or two after the loss, most of us experience the joyful memories more fully after a few years. In time, happy memories may be experienced more completely with less pain.

RITUAL

- Bake or buy the child's favorite cake and share it with family and friends.

- Celebrate the special gifts of your child by composing new words to the tune "Happy Birthday." Reflect on the words privately or share them with family and friends. For example:
  > Jon, we celebrate you
  > And the smile that we knew,
  > And the fun and the laughter
  > That we shared with you, too.

- Continue family birthday traditions such as eating at a favorite restaurant.

- Cover the two parts of a gift box—the lid and the bottom—with "Happy Birthday" wrapping paper. Place a bow on top of the package. Offer family members and friends the opportunity to recall special gifts the child shared with them. Gifts may be intangible, such as joy or laughter, or tangible, like a handmade key chain or a homemade card. Provide pieces of paper and pencils or pens and invite each person to write the "gift" on the slip. Place the papers inside the box and offer a prayer thanking God for the gift of your child.

- Light a candle in honor of the child and offer a prayer of thanks for the life of *name*.

READING

I will sing to the Lord, because he has dealt bountifully with me.

—Psalm 13:6

RESPONSE

We rejoice, Lord, in your gift of *name*, even as we mourn his or her loss. We celebrate his or her life and remember him or her with joy. Amen.

Cards

Have cards touched your life?

REFLECTION

We all like to know that others remember us. This is especially true when we suffer a great loss. Sometimes people do not know what to say, but they are able to send a card to let us know that they care. Personal notes in sympathy cards may be treasured forever because of the love and the warmth that they express. Each card, however, is also a reminder of the reality of our loss. While this may be good in some ways, it can also be painful to be reminded of it over and over.

Finding cards to send to others—e-greetings, hand-made, or purchased—may also remind us of our loss. Picking out cards for the birthday of other family members and friends may remind us of the one we are not going to send this year—or the next. The same may be true for other occasions like Christmas, graduation, and so on. Every trip to the card store can trigger reminders of the loss of our child.

When cards are received on special occasions like our own birthday, Easter, Mother's Day, or Father's Day, there will be one card that is conspicuous by its absence. For many people, it is a common practice to display all one's cards on a mantle or a table. Each time we look at such a display we may be reminded again of our loss. We may even fail to feel the expressions of love of friends and relatives because of overpowering feelings of grief. It may be important to remind ourselves of the care and the love expressed in the cards we have received.

Many parents save cards from their children. The first such written expressions of a child's love are precious. Those fathers and mothers who saved the cards they received from their daughters and sons have a lasting reminder that the bond of love between parents and children never dies. These treasures can bring back precious memories with a glance, but they can also remind us of our loss. Like all cards, they may elicit both joy and sorrow. For most of us, however, the good memories win in the long term and our lives are richer.

RITUAL

- Allow time for reflection when you make, order, or purchase greetings for others. Reflect on cards that would have made your child laugh, pictures that he or she would have enjoyed, and words that share the sentiments that you would like to express.

- Create a card for your child—even if it can never be sent. Draw or find a fitting picture, and attach or write appropriate words. Share your sentiments in this way at a birthday, holiday, or special event.

- Do something special with cards that you received from your child in the past. Add them to a memory box, create a collage, place them in a scrapbook, or store them in a drawer.

- Find the opportunity to read the printed, but especially the handwritten, messages in the "thinking of you" and "sympathy" cards that you have received. If desired, locate a special place to keep the greetings, but also give yourself permission to dispose of them when you are ready to give them up.

- Send cards to parents who have experienced the death of a child. Include acquaintances, co-workers, family members, friends, neighbors—and even total strangers. If possible, add a personal note or enclose a scripture passage or a special poem that has been meaningful to you.

READING

O that my words were written down!

O that they were inscribed in a book!

O that with an iron pen and with lead

they were engraved on a rock forever!

For I know that my Redeemer lives,

and that at the last he will stand upon the earth;

and after my skin has been thus destroyed,

then in my flesh I shall see God,

whom I shall see on my side,

and my eyes shall behold, and not another.
My heart faints within me!

—Job 19:23-27

RESPONSE

We thank you, God, for tangible expressions of love. We thank you for the knowledge that just as the bond of love between you and your children will never be broken, so also the bond between parent and child never changes. Amen.

Cemetery

How do you feel about visiting the cemetery?

REFLECTION

After the funeral most of us return periodically to the cemetery to remember our loved one. We may go to select a grave marker and choose the words that will be engraved on it. We may go to "decorate" or maintain the grave. We may return to simply visit and remember. Some of us return to talk to our loved one. Many of us feel much closer to him or her there. There is also comfort for many in the park-like atmosphere of cemeteries. If your child suffered terribly in life, it feels more like he or she is "resting in peace."

The frequency of our visits vary greatly from person to person, family to family, and culture to culture. Visits to the cemetery may even be affected by having to move out of town. Some go every week, others visit infrequently—if at all. We are all different. We all have different needs. This can be a source of conflict between spouses when one has a need to visit frequently because of the comfort it brings and the other feels only pain when at the cemetery. It is important to be aware of the feelings of others and to find the grace to accommodate their needs while meeting one's own.

A word to other children about cemetery visits can be important to them. You may wish to say that, although their brother or sister is not in the grave, but with Jesus, you still feel close to him or her there. Their brother or sister may not be here, but your love will never die. You might also wish to reassure your other children that they are just as important to you and that you will always love them, too.

RITUAL

- Consider visits to the cemetery—whether they are comfortable or uncomfortable to make—at certain times of the year including the anniversary of the death, a birthday, and on religious and secular holidays.

- Help younger children, as well as older ones, remember or tell the story of the life of their brother or sister. Stories could be shared before, during, or after a visit to the cemetery.

- Compare and contrast the New Testament's teachings, especially found in 1 Corinthians 15, about physical and spiritual bodies. All believers are promised life after death and bodies like Christ's (15:49)—resurrection bodies. Physical bodies die and decay, while resurrection bodies never die. Physical bodies might be sick and weak, but spiritual bodies are full of strength. Physical bodies are from the dust; resurrection bodies are from heaven.

- Observe the Jewish ritual of placing a stone of remembrance on top of the grave marker of the person who has died.

- Take time to design and select a grave marker that symbolizes the loving relationship with your child. When the marker is placed, hold a service of dedication that reflects the significance of the life and death of your loved one.

READING

So it is with the resurrection of the dead. What is sown is perishable, what is raised is imperishable. It is sown in dishonor, it is raised in glory. It is sown in weakness, it is raised in power. It is sown a physical body, it is raised a spiritual body. If there is a physical body, there is also a spiritual body (1 Corinthians 15:42-44).

RESPONSE

Our bodies may turn to dust, Lord, but our love lives on, just as our loved one lives on with you. As great as our love may be, your love is even stronger. For this we give you our thanks and praise. Amen.

Church

Do you find support at church?

REFLECTION

We come to church for many reasons. The main purpose is to worship. Some may come as individuals, but most of us come as families. When we sit in church we may know that we are there as God's family, but we are also accustomed to having our nuclear family around us. It may be very difficult to sit in the pew with one member of that family missing. We may find ourselves looking to see if he or she is standing or kneeling at appropriate times or we may discover ourselves finding the right page or searching for the offering for the missing child. In fact, it may be difficult to attend church at all—for mid-week activities as well as for Sunday services.

Some families may find it so difficult to attend without their child that they might consider changing parishes. While this may seem helpful to some, most families discover that this severs contact with a very important support system. We tend to make friends in our church—friends who are often a source of comfort and strength. In fact, there may be people in our own parish who have experienced the death of a child and who really do know what it feels like to lose a loved one. Furthermore, a sudden change may cause other children in the family to lose touch with an important source of stability such as their classmates, friends, and scout troop.

There may be many things in the life of a congregation that trigger grief. A child may have served as an acolyte, participated in the children's homily or the junior choir, and attended religious education classes or youth group events. There may be certain scripture passages or songs associated with his or her funeral. You may react to seeing your daughter's or son's friends and teachers or you may find that you have an unusually strong reaction to an announcement of a special outing for children or the sign-up brochure for summer camp programs. No two of us are the same. We may react to different things at church—even at different times—just as we do elsewhere. What is important to know is that these reactions are likely to occur—and that they are perfectly normal. God understands—and many members of the family of faith do, too.

RITUAL

- Give a gift for the worship space—such as an altar cloth or banner—as a memorial to your child.

- Go to church alone—or with another family member or a friend—to pray at a time other than the regularly scheduled masses or worship services.

- Make an appointment to talk with the pastor or another staff member about the mixed feelings you have about church. Take time to discuss the emotions associated with events such as confirmation or first communion or seasons like Christmas and Easter.

- Offer a prayer every time you enter or exit the church, such as "Thank you, God, for the memories of special times with *name of child* in your house of worship" or "Thank you, God, that *name of child* is part of your family of faith."

- Volunteer to help in the classroom of one of your other children or to assist with a special project like a seasonal event that involves your child's family or friends.

READING

The Lord is my light and my salvation;

whom shall I fear?

The Lord is the stronghold of my life;

of whom shall I be afraid?

One thing I asked of the Lord,

that will I seek after:

to live in the house of the Lord

all the days of my life,

to behold the beauty of the Lord,

and to inquire in his temple.

For he will hide me in his shelter

in the day of trouble;

he will conceal me under the cover of his tent;
he will set me high on a rock.

Hear, O Lord, when I cry aloud,
be gracious to me and answer me!
"Come," my heart says, "seek his face!"
your face, Lord, do I seek.
Do not hide your face from me.

Do not turn your servant away in anger,
you who have been my help.
Do not cast me off, do not forsake me,
O God of my salvation!
If my father and mother forsake me,
the Lord will take me up.

I believe that I shall see the goodness of the Lord
in the land of the living.
Wait for the Lord;
be strong, and let your heart take courage;
wait for the Lord!
—Psalm 27:1, 4-5, 7-10, 13-14

RESPONSE

Thank you, God, for the extended family of your church and for caring friends in the household of faith. May we find comfort in that family—and perhaps even be a comfort to someone else some day. Amen.

Church Year: Advent

Is Advent a time of darkness or light?

REFLECTION

Advent is a four week period of waiting for the birth of the Savior at Christmas. It is the season of the Christian year when we remember the long duration of time when people lived in the chaos and darkness of sin and longed for deliverance. All through the Old Testament, God's people saw and heard promises of what was to come. There were glimpses of "light at the end of the tunnel" as the prophets told about the one who was coming. These people lived in the hope that they would see the full light of God's love and peace, but the light didn't arrive until Jesus was born that first Christmas day.

Grief is a lot like Advent. There is an overwhelming feeling of chaos and darkness. There are hints and promises that things will be better some day. Sometimes we may even get a glimpse of the light as we experience good days or good moments, yet the darkness prevails. We hope for better times, for life to be normal, for pain to be gone. Yet it often seems that the darkness only gets deeper like the dark days of December at the time of the winter solstice. On the other hand, there is an old saying that "it's darkest just before the dawn."

Advent, the darkest time of the liturgical cycle, ends in the birth of the Light of the World. Our grief can be like that as well. In our deepest need, God reaches out to us and brings us hope and light. It may be in the words of a homily or a song, the kindness of a family member or a friend, a loving memory or a tangible treasure, or even the sharing of a stranger who has been where we are now. Advent is a time to remember that even in our darkest need, the Savior reaches out to us and brings us the light of Christ.

RITUAL

- Enhance the Advent season with candles. Bring a candle to someone who is waiting in a dark time in his or her life—a person who has recently lost a child or a lonely adult whose child died many years ago. In addition, visit a church where candles are burning and light one in memory of your child. Also, place a special candle in your home in honor of your loved one.

- Give a gift to enhance a waiting room in a doctor's office, hospital, mission, school, or transportation station. Suggestions include Advent devotions and readings, Bibles, and flowers or plants.

- Obtain information about a "Longest Night Service," which derives its name from the winter solstice, the darkest and longest night of the year, December 21.

The ritual is intended to minister to the needs of persons who are experiencing difficult times in their lives. Attend or start a "Longest Night" service in your community or congregation.

- Set up a family Advent wreath and review the importance of the candles, the circle, and the greenery. Read a passage related to "light" each week of Advent, such as Isaiah 9:2, John 1:1-9, John 8:12, and 1 John 1:5, 6. You may wish to use a study Bible or a Bible reference book to look up a list of prophecies and their fulfillment related to the birth of Jesus. Remember that just as God kept his promises in the past, God keeps his promises today, too.

READING

As long as I am in the world, I am the light of the world (John 9:5).

RESPONSE

Lord, help us to not be so blinded by the night that we fail to see your light in others or your word of hope. May we wait expectantly for dawn. Amen.

Church Year: Christmas

Is Christmas a mixed blessing?

REFLECTION

Christmas is a happy time of the year. We are surrounded by cards and cookies, gifts and greetings, Santa and singing. Christmas brings beauty, joy, light, and warmth into a time of the year that is otherwise dreary, dismal, dark, and cold. Christmas is eagerly awaited both in our Advent preparations and in the faces of people of all ages, but especially the children.

Much of what we associate with Christmas are things that are family oriented. There are family get-togethers, meals and parties, as well as shopping trips, tree decorating, cookie baking, stocking hanging, carol singing, and gift wrapping to name a few. Children participate in many of these activities in most families. When someone is missing from the fun and festivities it leaves a big gap. Whether the child was the "life of the party" or the "quiet one" who placed the angel or star on top of the family tree, or laid the Baby Jesus in the manger, that child's unique place in the family is unfilled. Family traditions like hanging ornaments, opening gifts, or viewing neighborhood lights are just not the same as they used to be.

On the other hand, there are things about Christmas that remind us of spiritual realities that can bring great comfort. We think of Jesus becoming a child like ours, sent to suffer and die for us—and we marvel at God's love. We remember the angels who celebrated Jesus' birth—and we wonder if they welcomed our dear child into heaven. We ponder the loving care Mary gave to her child—and we pray that she may be caring for our child also. We recall the tender mercy Joseph showed to his son—and we hope that he might be watching over our child as well. Use the twelve-day season of Christmas, December 25 through January 5, to observe the birth of the babe of Bethlehem in a meaningful way.

RITUAL

- Decorate a small tree with ornaments given or made by your child or with special memories of your daughter or son. Set it in a private place, such as a bedroom, or a public area like a family room or living room.

- Give a gift of food or funds to someone else. Bake or buy cookies and bring them to another family or parent who has lost a child, or donate money to an organization that purchases gifts for needy children.

- Look up a list of Old Testament prophecies and their New Testament fulfillment related to the birth of Jesus in a study Bible or Bible reference book. Remember God's steadfastness to people of Bible times and reflect on God's faithfulness to you today.

- Make a list contrasting the world without Jesus and the world with Jesus. Discuss the difference Jesus makes in your life.

- Ponder, like Mary, Christmas items that were significant in the life of your child—and that are still important in the experience of your family. Include things like ethnic traditions, favorite songs, handmade ornaments, special foods, and unique decorations. Reflect silently or with others or record feelings and thoughts in a journal.

READING

> In that region there were shepherds living in the fields, keeping watch over their flock by night. Then an angel of the Lord stood before them, and the glory of the Lord shone around them, and they were terrified. But the angel said to them, "Do not be afraid; for see—I am bringing you good news of great joy for all the people: to you is born this day in the city of David a Savior, who is the Messiah, the Lord" (Luke 2:8-11).

RESPONSE

Christmas is such a "mixed blessing," Lord. We celebrate the birth of your Son, and mourn the loss of our child. Help us to focus on the spiritual realities. Amen.

Church Year: Epiphany

What gifts do you celebrate at Epiphany?

REFLECTION

Epiphany means "appearance" or "revelation." Originally on January 6, now observed by many Churches on the Sunday after January 1, this festival celebrates the arrival of the magi, wise men who came from another country to bring gifts and worship to the Christ Child. Epiphany marks the revelation of the fact that Jesus, God's gift to us, is the Savior of the whole world, all nations and all peoples, not just the nation of Israel. The gifts these men brought represent "tribute" paid to a king. They are a way of indicating that this King is the greatest King. In some cultures families exchange presents on Epiphany instead of or in addition to Christmas Day as a way of remembering the arrival of the magi.

We can use Epiphany to celebrate the many gifts we have in our lives. We remember, of course, the gift of our Savior, but we can also rejoice in the gifts of Jesus' brothers and sisters who have helped us in our dark times by bringing a home-cooked meal or by offering a word of encouragement. We can rejoice in the lives of the saints who have taught us in their witness and their writings what it means to be a Christian. We can celebrate the fact that God gave us the gift of a child for a time—a child who enriched our lives and will never be forgotten. Hard as it may be, some of us may even be able to celebrate the process of our grief as a gift—a gift which helps us to adjust emotionally, physically, and spiritually to our loss.

RITUAL

- Consider giving a tangible gift, something of your child's that you have been reluctant to part with such as a book, doll, or sweater to someone who might need or enjoy it.

- Make a list of at least six ways that God's love has been and continues to be revealed to you. Ideas may include calls from friends, cards from strangers, casseroles from neighbors, concern from family, contacts from co-workers, and contributions from church members.

- Read Matthew 25:31-46 and use the season of Epiphany as a time to celebrate new revelations of God's presence among us through the hungry, thirsty, stranger, poor, sick, and imprisoned. Give a gift that will bring the light of Jesus' love into the lives of the people mentioned in this passage.

- Reflect on the intangible gifts your child shared with family and friends, such as goodness, honesty, kindness, joy, love, and warmth. Write the "gifts" on star-shaped pieces of paper and display them throughout the house or put them in inconspicuous places such as books or drawers to find from time to time.

• Volunteer for the presentation of the gifts at the Epiphany eucharist or the celebration of communion.

READING

> In the time of King Herod, after Jesus was born in Bethlehem of Judea, wise men from the East came to Jerusalem, asking, "Where is the child who has been born king of the Jews? For we observed his star at its rising, and have come to pay him homage." On entering the house, they saw the child with Mary his mother; and they knelt down and paid him homage. Then, opening their treasure chests, they offered him gifts of gold, frankincense, and myrrh (Matthew 2:1-2, 9-11).

RESPONSE

We pay homage to you, Lord, as our King—and as King of Kings. We remember all of your gifts to us and give thanks. Thank you especially for the gift of our dear child, *name*. Amen.

Church Year: Lent

What are your Lenten reflections?

REFLECTION

Lent is a forty day period of preparation for the celebration of Easter. Lent is generally observed as a time of fasting, prayer, and self-examination. During this season, there may be many reminders of your child, especially if he or she received the sign of the cross on Ash Wednesday, was old enough to be creative and personal about what he or she gave up for the Lenten fast, or participated in the parish's annual Palm Sunday procession. You may be reminded every time that you think of these things, as well as each time that you see others engaged in similar activities.

You may also be prompted to recall the distress of your child when you think of the anguish of our Lord. Your child may also have suffered. While Jesus' affliction and death was consciously chosen by him and served the higher purpose of our salvation, you may wonder what purpose the death of your child could possibly have served. It is one thing to choose death for the benefit of the human race; it is quite another to have your child taken from you by death. On the other hand, you may—for the first time—appreciate and identify the pain and suffering of Jesus, as well as that of Jesus' family and friends, especially his mother, Mary. Mary may not, at the time, have fully understood the significance of the loss of her child either. You may find that this gives new meaning to Lent for you.

There are other positive aspects to Lent as well. Each Sunday in Lent looks forward to Easter, where believers celebrate the joy of Jesus' resurrection and all that it means for us. It means that death is not the end. With Jesus we are and will be raised to new life—and not only us, but our children as well. Jesus rose to give victory over death to all his children. Lent points us to and prepares us to celebrate Jesus' victory which all who have gone before us share—saints, family, and friends.

RITUAL

- Choose a "thorny" concern that needs healing and offer it to God in prayer. Conduct a blessing for each family member by anointing each one with olive oil, making the sign of the cross, and speaking God's will for peace in their lives.

- Cut branches from an evergreen tree—a symbol of everlasting life—and fashion a cross to decorate the front door during the season of Lent.

- Keep a journal of changes observed during the weeks of Lent in both the outer, physical world and your inner, spiritual one.

- On Good Friday, take time to visit a church with the "Stations of the Cross." Remember that while the suffering of crucifixion and death can hardly be called "good," the atonement for sin and the gift of salvation through Christ's sacrifice is "Good News" for the Christian.

- Watch a video such as *Jesus of Nazareth* or *Jesus Christ, Superstar* to view the events of Jesus' suffering, death, and resurrection in a new way. Offer a prayer to God or write a letter to Jesus expressing your gratitude for the gift of salvation and eternal life.

READING

Jesus said to her, "I am the resurrection and the life. Those who believe in me, even though they die, will live, and everyone who lives and believes in me will never die. Do you believe this?" (John 11:25-26).

RESPONSE

We feel the pain of death and loss so strongly, Lord. We look forward to the day when we shall celebrate life forever. Amen.

Church Year: Easter

Do you claim God's promise of eternal life at Easter?

REFLECTION

Easter, the celebration of the resurrection of Jesus, is the day we remember Christ's victory over death. Because Jesus lives, we can be assured that we too shall live. Just as Jesus was raised from the dead, we will be raised to eternal—everlasting—life. Christ's resurrection is the first fruit of the promise made so long ago, the promise that we claim on this special day. And, as new members are received into the church during the Easter Vigil, we once again see the fruit of Jesus' resurrection in a visible way.

At Easter time many of us look around and see the much anticipated renewal of the earth as well. Flowers spring up out of the cold, "dead" ground. Leaves return to the trees. The air is warm again. All nature is fresh with the sights, smells, and sounds of spring. There is new life all around us.

At the same time that we see these signs of new life, we are reminded of the signs of our loss. There is a vacant spot at the table for Easter dinner. The fun of a hunt for hidden eggs is not as exciting as it used to be. There is one less holiday basket to prepare. The selection of new clothes—Easter outfits—isn't as enjoyable as it once was. Our grief colors even this most holy of days.

The message of Easter isn't that everything is perfect. The message of Easter is that, in spite of the imperfection of this world, everything will be perfect. Jesus' resurrection is in the past, but ours is still in the future. We celebrate because we know it is coming. Easter is a day to be reminded of God's promise—for our child, and for us.

RITUAL

- Attend an Easter Vigil or sunrise service that begins in darkness and ends in daylight. Reflect on God's promise to be with us during the "dark" and the "light" times of death and life.

- Color Easter eggs green and embellish them with symbols of everlasting life.

- Cut branches from an evergreen tree and create a cross to decorate the front door, or trim an evergreen tree with Easter symbols of new life.

- Reflect on the familiar images of Easter—bulb and blossom, seed and tree, cocoon and butterfly, cross and empty tomb—that remind us of the truth: the end is actually a new beginning. When a plant dies in the fall, all that is left is the dead-looking bulb. Yet in the spring, that bulb becomes a flower! When an apple falls to the ground, the outer layer rots away leaving only the seeds. In time, those seeds can produce new apple trees that blossom and bear more fruit! Although the caterpillar seems to die inside the cocoon, it becomes a new creature transformed into a beautiful butterfly! What seems to be the end each time becomes a new beginning! What looked like the end of Jesus' life as he died on the cross, was actually a new beginning for everyone. Jesus rose from the dead and promised that those who believe will have eternal life, too. That is the promise God makes to each one of us. That is the promise of Easter.

- Read or sing the words of favorite Easter hymns that proclaim a message of eternal life and resurrection. Listen to selections from Handel's *Messiah*, including the "Hallelujah Chorus" and "I Know That My Redeemer Liveth."

READING

But in fact Christ has been raised from the dead, the first fruits of those who have died. For since death came through a human being, the resurrection of the dead has also come through a human being; for as all die in Adam, so all will be made alive in Christ. But each in his own order: Christ the first fruits, then at his coming those who belong to Christ (1 Corinthians 15:20-23).

RESPONSE

Help us, Lord, to celebrate this Easter season. Jesus is alive. We give thanks for his resurrection—and for the certainty that all his children will also be raised. Amen.

Church Year: Pentecost

How do you experience the comfort of the Holy Spirit?

REFLECTION

Pentecost is the day we remember that the Holy Spirit was poured out on the church fifty days after Jesus' resurrection. On this Jewish harvest festival, the disciples were gathered in the upper room when a sound like wind permeated the space and what looked like tongues of fire appeared over their heads. Suddenly the disciples were filled with vigor and could speak in foreign languages. The Holy Spirit had come and infused them with the power of Jesus. Jesus' followers quickly went out to tell others the Good News of God's love and converted thousands to Christ in a single day. Just as God had lived with us in the human form of Christ, God now lives with us and in us in the form of the Holy Spirit.

Some might ask, "If God is in us and with us why didn't God prevent my child from dying?" There is no answer to that question that will satisfy the ache in your heart. Although God loves us very much, God does not take away all our pain, just as he did not take away Jesus' pain. In fact, God tells us that we will suffer a while. What God does promise is that he will be with us—in all circumstances of life. In fact, Jesus referred to the Holy Spirit as "the Comforter."

Sometimes when we are in pain a good friend will stay with us. He or she may not be able to take away our pain, but we are comforted in knowing that he or she is with us. The Holy Spirit is like that, always with us, holding our hand, as it were. This is what Jesus meant when he said, "I will never leave or forsake you," and "I will be with you always." We may be in pain, we may be angry, and our faith may be weak, but God is with us.

RITUAL

- Complete the phrase "I see red when. . . ." Since red is a color that is often associated with strong emotions, responses to the sentence might include, "I see red when people ask me if things are back to normal," or "I see red when people suggest that I should have another child," and "I see red when people tell me how I should feel." Also take time to consider that red, the liturgical color for Pentecost, symbolizes the fire of enthusiasm and the force of energy that God's empowerment brings.

- Look up Galatians 5:22-23, the passage that lists the "Fruits of the Spirit." Write the nine characteristics on a piece of paper. They include love, joy, peace, patience, kindness, generosity, faithfulness, gentleness, and self-control. Name at least one person—biblical, historical, or contemporary—who exemplifies the "Fruits of the Spirit" in his or her life and who serves as a mentor or a model of God's power and presence in your life.

- Page through a hymn book and locate songs that describe the person and work of the Holy Spirit. Titles might include "Breathe on Me, Breath of God" (Text: Edwin Hatch; Tune: Robert Jackson); "Every Time I Feel the Spirit" (African-American Spiritual); "The Spirit is A-Movin" (Carey Landry); "Spirit of the Living God" (Daniel Iverson), and "Lord, Send Out Your Spirit"(Joe Zisgray). Read or sing these messages and reflect on ways that you have experienced God's Spirit in your life.

- Read the story of Pentecost in Acts 2. Reflect on God's power and God's presence with the followers of Jesus who were gathered on that special day. Ask God to help you experience the Holy Spirit's power and presence in your life in a very real way, too.

- Reflect on biblical words for the Holy Spirit such as Advocate (John 14:16,17), Comforter (Luke 12:12), and Teacher (Luke 12:12). Write one or more references and words on a symbol of wind, such as a kite, pinwheel, or windsock, and display it as a reminder of God's presence through the Spirit.

READING

Likewise the Spirit helps us in our weakness; for we do not know how to pray as we ought, but that very Spirit intercedes with sighs too deep for words. And God, who searches the heart, knows what is the mind of the Spirit, because the Spirit intercedes for the saints according to the will of God (Romans 8:26-27).

RESPONSE

Thank you for the promise that you will always be with us. We don't always feel your presence, Lord, but it is a comfort to know that you are here. Amen.

Classmates/Friends/Teachers

How do you react when you meet people who were important to your child?

REFLECTION

Shopping at the grocery store or in the mall one day you meet your child's former teacher. That is not an unusual event for most parents. When you have lost a child, however, it may trigger many memories—good and bad. It may remind you of the love your child had for that teacher, or it may cause you to think of the countless conflicts they experienced. An unexpected meeting can be transformed into an emotional roller coaster ride. Unanticipated meetings can occur not only with a teacher, but also with classmates and friends. The warm feelings that come with good memories may linger or they may lead to depression because you realize that those good times are gone forever. The bad memories may lead to anger and a sense of frustration. On the positive side, a classmate, friend, or teacher may relate a story that affirms your child or that illustrates what a special person your daughter or son was.

A chance meeting with someone who knew your child, by its very nature, is unpredictable. Some meetings, however, are anticipated or planned in advance. These meetings can be much easier to handle because you have time to prepare yourself for what might occur. If you can prepare emotionally you are less likely to be caught off guard. Moments like going to school events with another child in the family can be easier to handle if you take time to rehearse in your mind what you will say or do when you meet people who were important in the life of the child you have lost. Because anticipated as well as unanticipated meetings will happen, take time to prepare for them in advance.

RITUAL

- Invite classmates, friends, and teachers to create a scrapbook of memories celebrating the life of your child. Provide pages of an album and ask participants to share pictures and stories of events that took place in and out of school.

- Keep a journal to reflect on ways that classmates, friends, and teachers affirm the qualities of your child.

- Practice responses to anticipated and unanticipated situations by rehearsing the reactions silently, speaking in front of a mirror, talking with a family member or friend, or writing the words on paper.

- Send a note of appreciation to school personnel such as cooks, custodians, librarians, nurses, principals, secretaries, and teachers thanking each person for the special role that he or she played in the life of your child.

- Write an A-Z poem. For every letter of the alphabet, list a feeling associated with planned and unplanned meetings with people who were important in the life of your child. Sentiments expressed could be positive or negative, or a combination of the two. For example, a positive emotion for the letter "A" might be "affirmed," while a negative reaction could be "appre-hensive." A positive feeling for "I" might be "invigor-ated," while a negative one could be "insecure."

READING

> No testing has overtaken you that is not common to everyone. God is faithful, and he will not let you be tested beyond your strength, but with the testing he will also provide the way out so that you may be able to endure it (1 Corinthians 10:13).

RESPONSE

Thank you, God, for the ability to mentally prepare for emotionally difficult moments—and for your grace to see us through those for which we cannot prepare. Amen.

Clock/Time of Day

*How do you remember the important
times or moments?*

REFLECTION

In today's world it seems like our lives are governed by the clock. We have alarm clocks, computer clocks, day timers, school schedules, wristwatches—and more. Clocks tell us when it is time to get up and when it is time to go to sleep. They tell us when we should eat, go to school or work, where we should be, what we can see on TV, and much more. Children are no less ruled by the clock than adults. They must be out the door by a certain time to catch the school bus—and they return at a certain time, day after day. They must be driven to games that start promptly at a specific time—or to dentist appointments, art, music, or dance lessons, Girl Scouts, Boy Scouts, and so forth and so on. Many parents know this schedule by heart. It becomes automatic. If it is Tuesday at 4:00 p.m., it is time to be at piano lessons. In addition to the clock on the wall, each of us has an internal clock. We know when it is time to get up in the morning, even without an alarm clock. We know when we are hungry, and when it's time for a meal or a snack. We know when it is time for our children to get off the bus.

Both of these clocks keep on ticking when we lose a child. The automatic response when we look at the clock in the early morning is to wake up the child who is no longer there in his or her bed. And even though we grieve our loss, when it is time for the bus to come in the afternoon we still expect him or her to come home. We catch ourselves and remind ourselves of the new state of reality. These moments can be jarring and painful, but they are not unexpected. Some of us have minds which can block such moments from consciousness, but for most of us they come uninvited to the front of our thoughts. A person who was so much of our life is not forgotten.

As time goes on, such moments may become less frequent. Our internal clocks can be "reprogrammed" by new schedules and different responsibilities. There may, however, always be those moments when we look at the clock and remember the important "times" in our lives.

RITUAL

- Acknowledge feelings and thoughts at different times throughout the day.

- Put a timepiece used by your child—such as a bedroom clock, a stop watch, or a wristwatch—in a special place in the home or in a memory box collection.

- Create a clock face to illustrate the way you might have spent a typical day with your child. Select a paper plate. With light pencil marks, divide the plate into fourths and place a small mark where the numbers 12, 3, 6, and 9 would appear, or as an alternative, divide the plate into twelve or twenty-four sections and mark each number at the appropriate point.

To make the clock personal, display unique illustrations representing how you spent your time. Choose a sticker, stamp, or magazine photo—or write words or draw pictures—representing daily events in your life. Add one illustration to each "number" mark on the circle.

Cut hands from heavy paper. Poke a hole through the bottom of the two hands and through the center of the plate. Push a brass paper fastener through the layers and then spread the brad from underneath to secure it in place. Set the clock to a special time of the day.

Cut or choose a piece of magnetic strip and affix it to the back of the clock. Attach the clock to your refrigerator or other magnetic surface. Each time you look at the measurement of time, remember that each moment is a gift from God.

- Start an "It's time to . . ." list. It might include things like call a friend to go to lunch, make an appointment with a counselor, or plan a special event with family members.

- Turn the routine of getting up in the morning and going to bed at night into a special time of prayer. When the alarm goes off, as well as when you set it, offer a prayer of thanks to God for the time you shared with your child.

READING

> Your kingdom is an everlasting kingdom,
>
> and your dominion endures throughout all
> generations.
>
> The Lord is faithful in all his words,
>
> and gracious in all his deeds.
>
> —Psalm 145:13

RESPONSE

Thank you, God, for the way that *name* was such an important part of our lives. Our memories are so pleasant, but our loss is painful. Help us from day to day to celebrate our time together. Amen.

Clothes

What should we do with the clothes?

REFLECTION

Clothes help us to define who we are and how we are seen by those around us. For a very young boy, a superhero shirt helps to convince him that he is a person with power(s) in a world where big people seem to have all the control. Teenagers find that their place in society—and often their popularity in school—is frequently determined in large part by how they dress. Gang members identify themselves by the way they wear a baseball cap or a pair of shoes. Executives "dress for success." Clothing symbolizes far more than its basic protective function might suggest. Perhaps that is why it is so difficult to dispose of clothes when a loved one dies.

Holding on to the clothes of your loved one is a way of holding on to much more than fabric. We hold on to an identity—a person. We hold on to smells. We hold on to memories. Parting with clothes makes our loss seem painfully real—and final. Cleaning out a closet and packing up clothes is usually one of the last things we do when we lose a loved one. Some of us experience giving away our loved one's clothes as an act of betrayal or disloyalty. Sooner or later there comes a time when we feel it is the right thing to do. Even then it is not easy. And, even then we may not want to part with everything. If we can, however, put items such as coats, hats, pants, shirts, skirts, shoes, sweaters, and more to good use, it serves a higher purpose.

RITUAL

* Compose a poem on the theme of protection—the protection provided by clothing, but more importantly, the security offered by God. Use the pattern for a "cinquain" poem, an unrhymed verse containing five lines and the following formula:

  Line 1: Two syllables for the topic

  Line 2: Four syllables describing the topic

  Line 3: Six syllables expressing action

  Line 4: Eight syllables expressing feeling

  Line 5: Two syllables that are a synonym for the topic.

For example, a cinquain related to clothing might be:

Clothing

Memories worn

Special places pictured

Very difficult to part with

T-shirts

A cinquain describing God's protection is:

Refuge

Security

Relying on God's care

Thankful for God's unfailing love

Faithful

- Create a "Memory Quilt" using pieces of your child's clothing—such as jeans or t-shirts—as the material for the project.

- Find the word "Sackcloth" in a Bible concordance and look up verses that illustrate how clothing was used in Bible times to symbolize mourning, for example: Genesis 37:34: Jacob rents his garments and puts on sackcloth when he thinks that his son Joseph is dead; Esther 4:1: Mordecai tears his clothes and puts on sackcloth to mourn the impending destruction of the Jewish people. Also look up verses that portray the use of clothing in connection with the resurrection, such as Matthew 27:35 and Revelation 3:5.

- Offer collections, such as hats, to classmates, cousins, or friends.

- Prepare a "Keepsake Box" of clothing from special occasions, such as a baptismal gown, a first communion dress, or a costume from a pageant or play.

READING

Of course, there is great gain in godliness combined with contentment; for we brought nothing into the world, so that we can take nothing out of it; but if we

have food and clothing, we will be content with these
(1 Timothy 6:6-8).

RESPONSE

It is difficult to say, "Goodbye," Lord. It reinforces the
finality of our loss. Help us to realize that *name* is not
his or her clothes, important though they were. May we
realize more fully that our treasure is with you. Amen.

Concerts, Performances, Plays, Recitals

Will you attend performances?

REFLECTION

Artistic activities are a big part of the life of many children. They range from choir festivals to vocal recitals, band concerts to orchestra performances, classroom skits to school plays, and dance exhibitions to twirling competitions. Some children may have been involved in these types of activities for many years while others could have just started. Since artistic endeavors are a big part of the life of many children, they are, consequently, a major part of the lives of their parents as well.

Preparation for an event can occupy much of the child's and the parents' resources. There is the time, as well as energy and money, spent in equipment, lessons, and rehearsals. There is the period spent chauffeuring children back and forth—or arranging for car pool drivers, drop off places, and pick up points. There is the rushing to get children, as well as equipment, ready for the instruction or lesson, and the waiting during the practice or rehearsal. Much time and effort are expended just preparing for the event itself—which can be over in minutes, hours, or days. When you have lost a child who was involved in such activities there is suddenly a vacuum in your life.

When the time comes for the actual performance in which your child would have participated there are other things to consider. Some groups may dedicate a performance to a member who has died. You may want to be present at such a memorial. Or you may want to attend, even if this is not done, as your own way of honoring your child. Other parents may not wish to go because the pain they feel is simply too great to bear. Still others may not wish to attend, but feel that they must because they have other children involved in the event. There may even be those parents who have been so deeply involved for many years that such performances have become a meaningful part of their own lives as well as the lives of their children. For them, staying home might not even appear to be an option. Each of us must consider our own needs as well as the needs of other family members when we make plans for our participation.

RITUAL

- Attend a concert, performance, play, or recital in honor of your child or to have your child honored. Support others—children in your family, young people in the group, as well as leaders and teachers, by participating in the program.

- Contribute an instrument, or other equipment or materials related to the activity, to someone who could use it or to someone who might not be able to afford to participate without this donation.

- Give a gift in memory of your daughter or son to support a drama or music program in the church, community, or school.

- Place an ad in the program in honor of the accomplishments of your child.

- Take time to listen to a recording or to watch a video of a performance in which your child participated. Reflect—alone or with others—on the pleasure, as well as the pain, that this activity brings to mind.

READING

For God alone my soul waits in silence;

from him comes my salvation.

He alone is my rock and my salvation,

my fortress; I shall never be shaken.

—Psalm 62:1-2

RESPONSE

Thank you, God, for the ways that cultural participation enriched the life of our child. Give us wisdom in making decisions about our own participation. Amen.

Court/Trial

Are there legal proceedings?

REFLECTION

Only those who have lost a child because of the actions of another person may know the pain that comes with legal proceedings. There may be a civil suit, criminal trial, or both. The pain of loss is made fresh with every deposition with an attorney, every discussion with a judge, every meeting with police, every picture in the press, and every interview with reporters. During the trial itself the facts are presented to the jury, along with graphic descriptions, disturbing details, terrible pictures, witness testimony, and victim impact statements. Through every step of the process, the story of your child's death is told over and over. The person who caused your child's death—intentionally or unintentionally—must be faced in the courtroom, often for days on end. The emotional wounds are opened again and again.

Beside the emotional costs, there are other costs as well. There are financial losses associated with a trial. There may be considerable time lost from work for appointments, hearings, meetings, and the trial itself. The amount of time necessary may cause considerable disruption to a career as well as to a family. There may also be expenses for child care, if you have other children, as well as for meals—since there's no time or energy to plan and prepare them. All in all, the costs can be exorbitant, both emotionally and financially.

On the positive side, a trial can help to answer questions that may arise in your mind. As evidence is presented, the causes of your child's death may become more clear. In spite of the pain a trial may bring, it might also help to bring closure to some of your unanswered questions and help to heal some open emotional wounds. A guilty verdict can be especially helpful, for it often brings with it the feeling that this part of one's pain is past. It offers the hope that one can now go on with the grieving process—and with rebuilding life—in some way.

RITUAL

- Carry an object—such as a pocket cross, a rosary, or an item of your child's—to remind you of God's presence during this difficult time.

- Establish a relationship with a prayer partner or a prayer chain—a group of people who call each other to share cares and concerns. Ask this person, or these people, to keep you and your family in their prayers all the time—but especially during the course of the emotionally, physically, and spiritually draining days of a trial.

- Express your need for assistance and take people up on offers of help for babysitting, errands, meals, and other tasks.

- Record facts, as well as feelings, in a journal that is kept throughout the process of a civil or criminal suit.

- Sustain yourself by having a support system in place before, during, and after legal proceedings. Invite people to be present during a trial, share cares and concerns with others who have had a similar experience, and talk with someone—personal friend or professional counselor—as an emotional release.

READING

Since, then, we have a great high priest who has passed through the heavens, Jesus, the Son of God, let us hold fast to our confession. For we do not have a high priest who is unable to sympathize with our weaknesses, but we have one who in every respect has been tested as we are, yet without sin. Let us therefore approach the throne of grace with boldness, so that we may receive mercy and find grace to help in time of need (Hebrews 4:14-16).

RESPONSE

Lord, you have shown yourself to us as a God who loves justice as well as mercy. Help us to bear the cost of justice and show us your mercy. Amen.

Dreams

Have you lost a dream?

REFLECTION

Most of us have dreams for our children. Our goals for our daughters and sons may be lofty or humble, large or small. Regardless of the size or the scope of our hopes, most parents have thought about their children's future. We may imagine them graduating from high school or college, getting married, and having children. We might dream of them being successful in their careers, jobs, or professions. Some of us may dream of our children following in our footsteps, while others may dream of them surpassing our achievements. On other levels, we may imagine our children becoming upstanding citizens or leaders of the community, nation, or world. We might also think of our children as showing outstanding moral courage like Dietrich Bonhoeffer, or deep spiritual commitment and compassion like Mother Teresa.

When we lose a child all of those unfulfilled hopes and dreams are lost as well. We may have precious memories of what he or she did achieve, but the future hopes and dreams are gone. We may see other children reach milestones in their lives only to be reminded of what could have been in the life of our child. We mourn not only our loved one, but all the dreams that are lost as well. What has happened is that we have come face to face with the fact that all of our dreams are subject to frustration. Whether they are dreams for our children or for ourselves, they may be gone like the morning mist. Some may be fulfilled, others will never happen. Those that are not may be mourned.

RITUAL

- Record the dreams that your child achieved. On a piece of paper, make a list of several accomplishments ranging from "took first step" to "ran a marathon," or "caught a ball" to "played on a team." Once the ideas are gathered, record your thoughts on a cassette tape. Place a blank tape into a recorder, and speak your reflections into the machine. Tranquil music could be played in the background. Consider inviting other family members and friends to add messages to the tape.

- Take time to visualize the dreams that you had for your child—personally and professionally. Include goals that were known only to you; embrace hopes that you never told anyone else. Using a wax crayon, draw pictures and print words representing the dreams on an 8 1/2" x 11" sheet of white paper. Use solid strokes to fill in the space. Dust the drawing with talc so paint will adhere to the picture. Cover the entire surface of the paper with black tempera paint. Allow the project to dry. At an appropriate time in the future, use the point of a pair of scissors to gently scrape away some of the black paint so that the dream will show through.

- Help someone fulfill a dream by offering a scholarship in a certain subject or to a specific school or by taking time to mentor or tutor a student.

- Acknowledge that some of your dreams for your child have been turned inside-out. Create a pillowcase with meaningful messages on the outside—or the inside—of the fabric. Think of your hopes in words and pictures and draw or write them on a piece of paper. (Note that letters must be printed in reverse to transfer onto the pillowcase.) Color the sketch with fabric crayons, pressing hard during the process. Place several layers of newspaper inside the pillowcase. Position the picture, drawing side down, on top of the material. Place a layer of paper towels over the illustration and iron over the design until the wax melts into the fabric. Remove the paper towel and notice that the picture is now permanently printed on the pillowcase. Share the reflections with others, or turn the pillowcase inside-out until you are ready to reveal some of your "dreams."

- Prepare jigsaw puzzle pieces containing dreams that your child accomplished and hopes that were never fulfilled. Blank jigsaw puzzles may be purchased, actual picture puzzles can be turned over so the blank, back side can be used, or shapes could be cut from manila file folders or poster board. Print one word or phrase associated with a dream on each piece. One or two pieces may be left blank or removed to suggest the dreams that were not achieved. Put the pieces together and celebrate the life of your child in the process.

READING

Come now, you who say, "Today or tomorrow we will go to such and such a town and spend a year there, doing business and making money." Yet you do not even know what tomorrow will bring. What is your life? For you are a mist that appears for a little while and then vanishes. Instead you ought to say, "If the Lord wishes, we will live and do this or that" (James 4:13-15).

RESPONSE

Lord, many people cannot even imagine the pain of losing a dream. For some of us it is all too real. Help us to realize that all of our dreams are ephemeral and may never be realized. And help us to trust in your love and care. Amen.

Driver's License

Is it time for the driver's license?

REFLECTION

Sixteen years old. A magical time for a child. The time when—in most states—he or she is first eligible for a driver's license. The driver's license is something of a rite of passage that brings joy to a child—and dread and fear to many parents. If your child died before turning sixteen, however, it may bring other emotions. When you see his or her classmates driving down the street it may trigger thoughts of your child and the experience that he or she is missing. You may imagine the elation that would have come with getting that license, or you may wonder if the responsibility that goes with driving may have aroused a little apprehension.

Seeing a car with a "student driver" sign may cause you to wonder if people would give a wider berth to your child as you do for other students. The thought that you do not have to worry about your child driving, that you do not have to wait in line at the Bureau of Motor Vehicles, or that you do not have to pay high insurance premiums is not much consolation. You would undoubtedly trade all of those things just to have your son or daughter back for a single day.

If your child died shortly before his or her sixteenth birthday, you will experience one set of emotions. If your child died much earlier, your thoughts and feelings may be quite different. You may, for example, wonder what kind of a sixteen-year-old he or she would have been. Polite and respectful? Or rebellious and rude? Perhaps, like most teenagers, a little of both? Most of us cannot help but wonder, "What would he or she be like today?"

Some may find thoughts like these comforting. Many of us find them to be frustrating. We only know for certain what was and what is, not what might have been. We know the joy our child brought us. We know that he or she is a child of the God who loved him or her enough to send Jesus. If we become frustrated with wondering what "might have been," we can remind ourselves to center our thoughts on the things we know.

RITUAL

- Buy a new keyring to commemorate the day that your child could have received his or her driver's license. Keep it for yourself or give it to your spouse as a remembrance of the event.

- Imagine your daughter or son getting a license and driving a car. Visualize the kind of car he could have had, the places she might have gone, the passengers in the vehicle, and anything else that comes to mind.

- Keep a journal of "Rites of Passages" and record thoughts and feelings at the times various rituals could have occurred in your child's life.

- Offer a prayer for the students—and the instructor— each time you pass a "Driver's Training" vehicle.

- Purchase car wash coupons, or other automobile-related items, and give them as gifts to your child's friends when they receive their driver's licenses.

READING

For God has destined us not for wrath but for obtaining salvation through our Lord Jesus Christ, who died for us, so that whether we are awake or asleep we may live with him. Therefore encourage one another and build up each other, as indeed you are doing (1 Thessalonians 5:9-11).

RESPONSE

Help us, Lord, to remember that our child is also your child. We may never know what might have been, but we can be sure that *name* belongs to you. Thank you for that assurance. Amen.

Emergency Vehicles

How do you respond to emergency vehicles?

REFLECTION

Emergency vehicles—ambulances, fire trucks, and police cars—pass you on the road, their lights flashing and their sirens screaming. You may see them as you drive down the street to or from church or the grocery store, or as you are on the highway during a longer trip. Emergency vehicles may go past your house or through your neighborhood on a daily basis. They are virtually unavoidable. One can't help wonder where they are going and what has happened. Was someone hurt? Will the person, or people, live—or die? It is human nature to be fascinated by ambulances, fire trucks, and police cars, to be curious. If the vehicle stops nearby, most of us gather to watch and see what takes place. People peer through their windows, come out of their houses, or stop their cars—and usually gawk.

When we are on the receiving end of the work of emergency personnel our perspective is quite different, of course. We may be sick or injured, have lost our car to an accident, or be involved in a house fire. At those times we see the lights and sirens in a rather different way.

You also see them quite differently when you have lost a child to accident, assault, injury, fire, or critical illness and have used the services of emergency personnel and emergency vehicles. Seeing the lights and hearing the sirens may bring back painful memories in a fraction of a second. You may, in a very real way, relive the experience with all its emotions, both positive and negative. It may take all of a person's coping skills just to get through the experience at times. One thing that helps many people cope is to remember the dedicated individuals who serve in emergency situations. Many of them risk their lives daily and have committed themselves to serving others. Focusing on their dedication, care, and concern may give new meaning to those lights and sirens—and the way they may have helped your child and your family.

RITUAL

- Choose a holiday—often a work day for emergency personnel—to remember the dedication of ambulance, fire, and police crews. Bring a cake, make a visit, or send a card to express appreciation for their services.

- Learn a variety of relaxation techniques, such as breathing exercises, to use in stressful situations.

- Organize a Teddy Bear collection and donate the stuffed animals to emergency crews—especially police officers—to give to children involved in traumatic situations.

- Pray for emergency personnel on a regular basis. Add this petition to a daily prayer list or remember these people at a special time every day.

- Respond to the flashing lights or screaming sirens of emergency vehicles by offering a prayer for the person and the family involved in the traumatic situation.

READING

God is our refuge and strength, a very present help in trouble.

—Psalm 46:1

RESPONSE

We are thankful, Lord, that you are always there for us. Thank you for providing the people who dedicate themselves to protecting us and helping when we are in need. Amen.

Family Picture/Portrait

Is it time for a family picture?

REFLECTION

At some time after the loss of a child most families will come to a point where they will want to have another family portrait taken. Although many will try to put this moment off as long as possible, other children grow up and change in appearance. Many parents will want to have a portrait made before older children go off to school in another town or before the marriage of a son or a daughter. There may also be occasions which "require" a portrait such as an anniversary, church directory, or Christmas card. Less formal occasions will occur such as birthdays and vacations which involve family pictures.

It may be difficult to have such a picture taken because of the reality that someone is missing. The permanence of your loss is reinforced by the fact that your whole family is not there. You are reminded of this even after the portrait is taken since you can't help but notice the absence of one of your children—or your only child— every time you look at the picture. There is a void in the picture—as well as in your heart. You may find it helpful at times like these to remind yourself that the photo only portrays part of your family. You may be apart, separated from your child for a time, but you are still a family.

RITUAL

- Address the dynamics of the situation before you pose for a family picture. Discuss arrangements, such as placement of people, with family members as well as with the photographer before the event takes place.

- Ask other families who have lost a child how they handled the first family portrait after the death of their daughter or son.

- Imagine your family reunion in heaven and draw a picture to illustrate the scene.

- Include a subtle reminder of your child in a "formal" portrait. Hold your child's doll or teddy bear on your lap, place a picture of your child on a table or a wall in the background, or wear a piece of jewelry that belonged to your child or that was given to you by your child.

- Place a different focus on a formal family portrait. Have the picture taken the "opposite" of the way it was usually done—go outside rather than inside, stand instead of sit, or wear casual clothes rather than your "Sunday best."

READING

Then I saw a new heaven and a new earth; for the first heaven and the first earth had passed away, and the sea was no more. And I saw the holy city, the new Jerusalem, coming down out of heaven from God, prepared as a bride adorned for her husband. And I heard a loud voice from the throne saying, "See, the home of God is among mortals. He will dwell with them as their God; they will be his people, and God himself will be with them; he will wipe every tear from their eyes. Death will be no more; mourning and crying and pain will be no more, for the first things have passed away." And the one who was seated on the throne said, "See, I am making all things new." And he said, "Write this, for these words are trustworthy and true." Then he said to me, "It is done! I am the Alpha and the Omega, the beginning and the end. To the thirsty I will give water as a gift from the spring of the water of life. Those who conquer will inherit these things, and I will be their God and they will be my children" (Revelation 21:1-7).

RESPONSE

Lord, we miss *name* so much that it is difficult to remember that our family will be complete again some day. Be with us while we grieve our separation and take care of *name* for us. Amen.

Graduation

How will you face graduation?

REFLECTION

Graduation is a very special time—whether it is graduation from pre-school, kindergarten, middle school, high school, college, or university. In addition to the graduation ceremony and possibly a baccalaureate service, there may be awards or honors banquets, events, parties, and, of course, the prom. All of these times evoke memories in parents. For some parents, those memories may be of their own graduation. For parents who have lost a child, those memories may more often be of their child.

For those who lost a child before graduation, there is the pain of watching other people's children graduate—and thinking about what might have been. All the advertising and merchandising associated with graduation presents constant reminders that someone is missing. Some classes may dedicate the ceremony—or a yearbook—to the memory of a student. Parents may be invited to the event or to a memorial service for their son or daughter. Parents may even be asked to accept an award or a diploma on behalf of their child. Some parents may have to ask God for special grace to be present at such events.

Some of us may have lost a child during events connected with graduation. Occasionally children die in accidents the night of the prom or in celebrations the day after graduation ceremonies. This turns what is supposed to be a happy, joyful time in the life of a child—and his or her parents—into a great tragedy. It may make the graduation time of younger siblings a period of intense anxiety for parents. There may even be fear as the children of close friends and relatives approach the end of their school career. Sharing those fears with friends or loved ones often makes them more manageable.

RITUAL

- Consider the theme of your child's "graduation" from death to eternal life with God. Take time to ponder the "ceremony" of meeting God, Jesus, and "graduates" from all times and places in heaven.

- Donate a plant or floral arrangement to a church or school in honor of the day that your child would have graduated. Or, purchase cut flowers or a dish garden for your own home or to give as a gift to a favorite school counselor, principal, or teacher.

- Hold a gathering or party at the time that your child would have graduated. Invite family members and friends to share in a celebration of the life of your child.

- Pose a series of "I wonder" questions related to the theme of graduation—in writing in a journal, silently in your mind, or verbally with another person or group. Examples might include, "I wonder if my child would have ranked in the top ten in the class," "I wonder who would have been his or her prom date," or "I wonder if my child would have received a scholarship."

• Send cards or notes of congratulations to friends of your child at the time of their graduation.

READING

When Jesus saw the crowds, he went up the mountain; and after he sat down, his disciples came to him. Then he began to speak, and taught them, saying:
"Blessed are the poor in spirit, for theirs is the kingdom of heaven.

"Blessed are those who mourn, for they will be comforted.

"Blessed are the meek, for they will inherit the earth.

"Blessed are those who hunger and thirst for righteousness, for they will be filled.

"Blessed are the merciful, for they will receive mercy.

"Blessed are the pure in heart, for they will see God.

"Blessed are the peacemakers, for they will be called children of God.

"Blessed are those who are persecuted for righteousness' sake, for theirs is the kingdom of heaven.

"Blessed are you when people revile you and persecute you and utter all kinds of evil against you falsely on my account. Rejoice and be glad, for your reward is great in heaven, for in the same way they persecuted the prophets who were before you" (Matthew 5:1-12).

RESPONSE

Graduations are not a time for celebration for some of us, Lord. They have become a time to think about what "might have been." Help us to focus on what is— your love and your faithfulness. Amen.

Hobbies

Did your daughter or son have a hobby?

REFLECTION

Hobbies fill many needs in our lives. They can be a way to socialize, or a way to be alone. They can be a quest for knowledge or skill, or a way to pass the time. Hobbies can be a means to express creativity, or a way to escape from reality. They can be a statement of individuality, or a way of belonging to a larger group. For many people hobbies are central to their identity. Hobbies are often a very important part of life, and hobbies can be a very important part of the life of a child.

When a child dies, however, his or her involvement in a hobby has many implications. First, there is all the "stuff." What do parents do with the tangible part of a hobby—baseball cards, dolls, model airplanes, paints, stamps, and so forth? Seeing the items around may be difficult, or it may be a symbol of the vitality of his or her life and, consequently, something to be treasured. If you shared the hobby with the child it may be painful to continue the hobby since every moment you spend reminds you of your loss. On the other hand, keeping a hobby may be a way to feel close to the child because it was important to him or her. In addition, other children should be considered before deciding what to do with "hobby stuff." Another child may want to take up the hobby as a way of staying in "contact" with the brother or sister that died. Hobbies can still fill needs— in many lives and in many ways.

RITUAL

- Consider donating the tangible portion of a hobby to a club or organization so other children may have the opportunity to develop their skills.

- Create a booklet of memories related to a child's hobby. Cut paper into 6″ x 18″ pieces and match two of the short ends. Place the ends together but do not overlap the paper. Carefully tape the paper to form a 6″ x 36″ strip. Fan-fold the strip into eight equal sections. Letter the name of your child and words related to her or his hobby on the top section. Add information and illustrations to each page. Tie a ribbon around the finished project. Keep the book in a special place as a reminder of the hobby and share it with family and friends from time to time.

- Hold a private or a public display of your child's hobby. Take time to enjoy his or her accomplishments or interests before deciding what to do with the items.

- If the hobby was shared by both child and parent(s), consider mentoring or teaching someone else who is already involved or who might like to get involved with the interest. Contact a community organization or a school for information or involvement regarding a project.

- Start a new hobby—alone or with other people. Discuss options with a spouse, other family members, friends, or co-workers and explore a new pastime.

READING

So, whether you eat or drink, or whatever you do, do everything for the glory of God (1 Corinthians 10:31).

RESPONSE

Thank you, God, for the little things in life that bring us joy. Thank you for the fun that *name* had with his or her hobby. Thank you for good memories. Amen.

Holidays: Halloween

Are you wearing a mask?

REFLECTION

Halloween is such a fun holiday, second only to Christmas in its popularity with children—and in the amount of money spent on all aspects of the celebration. Candy and costumes appear in stores months before the big day. Children anticipate trick-or-treating—or the local substitute, the fall fling or the harvest happening. Boys and girls, as well as older youth, make elaborate plans for their costumes. Will they be a ballerina, a ghost, a superhero, or the star of the current movie fad? Then, finally, the big day arrives. Decorations are prevalent. People of all ages are festive. Children go from house to house to gather goodies. Classes and clubs, as well as family and friends, throw parties. It is the time of the year to carve pumpkins and to make caramel apples. It is also another time of the year to remember that your child is missing—and that you are missing your child.

Halloween is a holiday when everyone seems to be pretending to be someone or something they are not, hiding behind costumes, make-up, and masks. That makes it easier for some of us to pretend to be happy, to make-believe that everything is all right. It's hard not to think about the parties and the fun that will be missed, and the festiveness of the season may help to hide our pain, for good or for bad. Concentrating on other children's excitement helps to deny our own loss. Halloween might be a good time to remember to take off the mask for a while and let someone see who we really are and what we are truly feeling on the inside—as well as the outside. God already knows.

RITUAL

- Decorate the inside or the outside of the house—simply or elaborately—using the theme of your child's favorite Halloween character or costume.

- Make or purchase a plain mask, such as one that covers the eyes rather than the full face. Read the words of Psalm 139 in its entirety, as well as by verse and stanza. Reflect on things that you are trying to hide, and print descriptive words on the inside of the disguise. Ponder some of the things that cannot be hidden from God and write reminders of them on the outside of the mask. Remember that God knows everything about us—and cares for us at all times and in all ways.

- Offer to take a child to a party or to go trick-or-treating. It might be someone whose parent is out of town on business, a young person whose mom or dad has to work, or a boy or girl in a household with a new baby or a sick family member.

- Select a colleague, counselor, family member, or friend and "unmask." Rather than covering up an emotion, take a risk and share a feeling with someone you can trust.

- Volunteer to help an association that offers neighborhood watch or an organization that checks candy on Halloween night.

READING

O Lord, you have searched me and know me.

You know when I sit down and when I rise up;

you discern my thoughts from far away.

You search out my path and my lying down,

and are acquainted with all my ways.

Even before a word is on my tongue,

O Lord, you know it completely.

You hem me in, behind and before,

and lay your hand upon me.

Such knowledge is too wonderful for me;

it is so high that I cannot attain it.

Where can I go from your spirit?

Or where can I flee from your presence?

If I ascend to heaven, you are there;

if I make my bed in Sheol, you are there.

If I take the winds of the morning

and settle at the farthest limits of the sea,

even there your hand shall lead me,

and your right hand shall hold me fast.

If I say, "Surely the darkness shall cover me,

and the light around me become night,"

even the darkness is not dark to you;

the night is as bright as the day,

for darkness is as light to you.

For it was you who formed my inward parts;

you knit me together in my mother's womb.

I praise you, for I am fearfully and wonderfully
made.

Wonderful are your works;

that I know very well.

My frame was not hidden from you,

when I was being made in secret,

intricately woven in the depths of the earth.

Your eyes beheld my unformed substance.

In your book were written

all the days that were formed for me,

when none of them as yet existed.

How weighty to me are your thoughts, O God!

How vast the sum of them!

I try to count them—they are more than the sand;

I come to the end—I am still with you.

—Psalm 139:1-18

RESPONSE

You know us inside and out, Lord. No masks, no pretending. At times masks are so useful for hiding from others, but there is no need to hide from you, even if we could. Thank you for your love, regardless of how we feel. Amen.

Holidays: Mother's Day and Father's Day

Will there be Mother's Day or Father's Day celebrations?

REFLECTION

Mother's Day and Father's Day are not major holidays, but they are annual observances that are packed with emotional importance. This is especially true for those who have lost a child. There may be banquets at one's church, parties at the club, or events at a school. No matter how many children a father or mother might have, it may be difficult to attend such functions and to see others there with their families intact. There are also the usual family gatherings, of immediate and extended relatives, where there is obviously someone missing. And, there are also the constant reminders such as the missing call, card, flowers, or gift. If one has lost an only child there is a vast feeling of emptiness, and if you are an older parent there is the fact that there is no one to call or visit.

Some parents may experience other emotions on these days as well. There may be guilt because of the fact that none of us are perfect parents. Some may dwell on their shortcomings and feel a burden of guilt. Parents may bring up and dwell on the things they wish they had done differently in raising their child. Some who lost a daughter or a son to illness and had to make difficult choices for their child's care may wonder if they made the right decisions. What many of us forget is that we nearly always make the best choices that we can for our children. Given what we know at the time and our own capabilities, we tend to be the best parents we can be. We can seldom do better than that. God knows that we are not perfect and God knows that we try our best. God also forgives us when we fail. We must also learn to forgive ourselves.

RITUAL

- Journal responses to sentence starters such as "I'm glad. . . ." "I'm grateful. . . ." or "I wish. . . ."

- Take time to consider answers to questions people commonly ask such as "How many children do you have?" or "Is the whole family getting together on Mother's Day or Father's Day?"

- Create a "God's File" from a folder or storage container. Write on slips of paper any anxieties that are related to the observance of Mother's Day or Father's Day, for example, "I should have spent more time with my child," or "Will anybody invite me for dinner?" Place the slips of paper in "God's File," surrendering the concern to God. Plan to review the file next year to see how God has worked in your life.

- Encourage young fathers and mothers to develop their parenting skills by offering a gift such as a book, a class, or time to be together.

- Write a "change" poem to reflect the "change" that has taken place in your family. Begin with one noun, then write descriptive phrases that lead the noun to "change" to another. For example:
  Child
  born into our family
  brought joy to life
  injured in accident
  entered eternal life
  child of God.

READING

For this reason I bow my knees before the Father, from whom every family in heaven and on earth takes its name. I pray that, according to the riches of his glory, he may grant that you may be strengthened in your inner being with power through his Spirit, and that Christ may dwell in your hearts through faith, as you are being rooted and grounded in love. I pray that you may have the power to comprehend, with all the saints, what is the breadth and length and height and depth, and to know the love of Christ that surpasses knowledge, so that you may be filled with all the fullness of God.

Now to him who by the power at work within us is able to accomplish abundantly far more than all we can ask or imagine, to him be glory in the church and in Christ Jesus to all generations, forever and ever. Amen (Ephesians 3:14-21).

RESPONSE

Lord, the warm feelings of Mother's Day and Father's Day can be hard to come by at times. Help us to remember the good times and the love we shared as parent and child. And help us to forgive ourselves when necessary, just as you forgive us. Amen.

Holidays: New Year

Will it be a "Happy" New Year?

REFLECTION

The new year is traditionally a time for looking back and for looking ahead. It is a time for putting the past behind us and for celebrating the adventure of a new year. Looking in either direction is less than exciting to someone who has lost a child, and yet it is something that must be done. Looking back is quite different for those who have lost a loved one. It can be a time when grief is renewed and re-experienced. Looking ahead is less than a celebration. It is more like an anticipation of dread. Yet both can be used as part of our grieving process.

Looking back can be a time to review good memories as well as an occasion to grieve. When friends and loved ones gather, we can pause to rejoice in the life of our child. Looking forward may be somewhat more difficult as it is a future without someone who is dear to us. Even, however, with the uncertainties that the future holds, we know Who holds the future. As Christians, we can be certain that the God who loves us and understands our suffering will be with us and sustain us. Many people have gone through the same kind of pain we are experiencing. A number of them have discovered that God has used their pain for something good. There is no way for us to know if that will be our experience, but we can know that we are in the hands of the One who cares for our every need.

RITUAL

- Go for a prayer ride or walk—individually, as a couple, an immediate or extended family, or a group of friends or neighbors. On New Year's Day—or soon after—gather outside your residence and pray that God's blessing will rest on your home in the next 365 days. Then drive or walk to places that were important in the life of your child, such as church, library, nature center, school, sports field, and so forth, and repeat the process in each location.

- Locate the song "O God, Our Help in Ages Past" in a hymnal. Its message, written by Isaac Watts in 1719, is that God's love comes before us, is with us now, and will go on forever. Read the words of the hymn and remember that God's love is always present, has always been present, and will always be present. God can lead us today—and tomorrow—just as God has led us in the past.

- Make New Year's resolutions that involve goals such as getting involved in a specific cause, researching support groups, or sorting through pictures. Write the resolution on a magnet and affix it to a place—such as a refrigerator door—where it will be seen every day.

- Select a calendar for the new year that reflects a favorite interest of your child such as cartoons, dogs, or sports, or make a calendar using special pictures for each month. Use seven pieces of paper for the calendar. Although the paper can be any size, a large size such as 11" x 17" allows room to create interesting illustrations on the pages. Fold the seven pages in half, and staple the sheets in the middle, on the crease line. Use the twelve top sections of the calendar to depict a memory related to the month. To make the pages for each month, dates may be copied off of another calendar, or calendar pages may be duplicated and glued to the bottom of each respective sheet. Design a cover to complete the project.

- Use the following Litany as part of a New Year's Eve or a New Year's Day gathering of family and friends.

  Leader: God of new beginnings, we rejoice that despite our fears and anxieties we may approach a new year with hope . . .

  All: for your steadfast love endures forever.

  Leader: God of the ages, who brought time into being, grant that we may view our lives with an eternal perspective . . .

  All: for your steadfast love endures forever.

  Leader: God of our tomorrows, longing for a fresh start, we bring you our past and trust in your renewing power . . .

  All: for your steadfast love endures forever.

Leader: God of eternity, we offer you both our past and our future, placing our lives in your presence . . .

All: for your steadfast love endures forever.

READING

But those who wait for the Lord shall renew their strength, they shall mount up with wings like eagles, they shall run and not be weary, they shall walk and not faint (Isaiah 40:31).

RESPONSE

Help us, Lord, in this time when everyone is celebrating. Help us to realize that we also have things to celebrate, even though our celebration may be quite different. You have been with us through the pain of the past. May we feel your presence in the coming year and take comfort in your love and care. Amen.

Holidays: Patriotic

Do patriotic holidays have special meaning?

REFLECTION

Patriotic holidays are times when we remember the sacrifice made by those who have given their lives in service to their country. For many, these occasions, especially Memorial Day, Fourth of July, or Veterans Day, involve a trip to the cemetery to place flowers on a grave. While this expression of love may be comforting to most of us, it can also cause our grief to well up inside once again. Each of us is somewhat different in this regard. For many this ritual is a positive experience, an expression of love and devotion, a way of saying, "I will never forget you."

If you have lost one or more family members in military service, a patriotic holiday might mean a great deal more to you because it is a day when the entire city, region, state, and nation remember your child's sacrifice. The day is a way of honoring your daughter or son, but it may also be an occasion for your grief to rise to the surface whether or not you choose to visit the cemetery.

Then there are the parades. For most people, especially children, parades are happy events. Folks enjoy the floats, the marching bands, the military drill teams, and the colorful units of every sort. Even the children of those who were lost in war may not connect the death of their parent with the parade or the holiday it celebrates. Their excitement may contrast with your feelings, even to the point where you are asked, "Why are you crying, Dad or Mom, or Grandma or Grandpa?" What one responds to a question like this depends both on your own needs and how much you think your child or grandchild can comprehend. You should consider both your needs and the child's before you answer.

RITUAL

- Attend a community event such as a memorial in the cemetery, a parade in the community, or a salute in the park with children—daughters, sons, grandchildren, nieces, or nephews. Take time to share stories of the relative who lost her or his life during military service.

- Display an American flag in honor of the life of your daughter or son and your child's service to her or his country.

- Read or sing the words of patriotic hymns such as "America the Beautiful," "The Battle Hymn of the Republic," and "My Country 'Tis of Thee." Offer a prayer of thanks for all who have given their lives in service to their country. Remember other families that mourn the loss of a daughter or a son on a patriotic holiday.

- Spend time looking through memorabilia connected with your child's military service—items such as awards, letters, medals, pictures, and uniforms. Reflect on this portion of your child's life—alone or with others.

- Visit the cemetery on a patriotic holiday and place a special expression of respect on the grave of your loved one.

READING

May the Lord give strength to his people!

May the Lord bless his people with peace!

—Psalm 29:11

RESPONSE

Thank you, God, for days when we all remember those who have died for our country. Give peace to their souls and peace to our land. Amen.

Holidays: Thanksgiving

How will you give thanks?

REFLECTION

Turkeys, pumpkins, feasting until we burst—these are all things we associate with Thanksgiving Day in our culture. Perhaps the one thing we most identify with Thanksgiving is the family gathering for dinner. We are supposed to give thanks, but that is difficult when there is a child missing from the family circle. How can we give thanks in the midst of grief? The Pilgrims faced that exact question.

The first Thanksgiving celebration took place less than one year after most of the Pilgrims—including children—had died from illness and starvation. The community knew that the rest would perish the following winter if the colony was not blessed with a good harvest. They could have given up in despair, but they struggled on in spite of deprivation. They willed themselves to survive, with God's help. They could have focused only on what they had lost, but they took a day to stop and focus on what they had gained.

Certainly the Pilgrims grieved for those who had died. They were as human as the rest of us. They took a moment, however, to acknowledge that although they had lost much, they had also received some blessings. Although our lives may not be as dramatic as those of the Pilgrims, we, too, have received blessings—even in the midst of our grief. Perhaps we can take a moment to focus on them and celebrate them for a time. We may discover that God gives us the grace to choose to make it a habit.

RITUAL

- Fill a cornucopia—a horn of plenty—with items that belonged to your child or with objects or pictures that remind you of your child. As each one is placed in the display, take time to reflect on the blessings that your child brought—and still brings—to you, as well as to others. Use the cornucopia as a Thanksgiving center-piece or decoration.

- Make or purchase a magnet depicting a Thanksgiving symbol such as a horn of plenty or a Pilgrim. Display the magnet year-round as a reminder to be grateful for God's blessings—small and large—every day, not just once a year.

- Reflect on the words of the Thanksgiving hymn, "Now Thank We All Our God," written by Martin Rinkart in 1647. Remember that the words were composed at a trying time in history, during the long conflict called "The Thirty Years' War." Martin Rinkart, a Lutheran minister, was conducting forty to fifty funerals each day—including services for his own family members.

Despite the difficulties, Martin took time to pray and sing God's praises. When the Thirty Years' War was finally over, every church was ordered to hold a thanksgiving service. As Martin read the words of 1 Thessalonians 5:16-18 he was inspired to write the text which became the hymn, "Now Thank We All Our God." The story of Martin Rinkart can remind us that whether times are good or bad, we can turn to God and give thanks.

- Review the legend of the "Five Kernels of Corn." During the Pilgrim's first winter in America, the weather was very cold and food was in short supply. Quantities of corn were so depleted that only five kernels were rationed to each person each day. When spring finally came, the Pilgrims, with the help of the Native Americans, planted crops and grew food. Harvesting vegetables, such as corn, saved them from starvation, and fortunately, many survived the hardship. According to an old New England custom, the Pilgrims wanted their children to remember the sacrifice and the suffering that made the new settlement possible. From then on, at Thanksgiving, the Pilgrims put five kernels of corn on each plate and used them to remind themselves of their blessings. Each kernel was employed to express gratitude to God for a different type of bounty: First kernel: autumn beauty; second kernel: family; third kernel: God's love and care; fourth kernel: friends; fifth kernel: freedom. Distribute five kernels of corn to each participant and take time to use the Pilgrim's method of expressing thanks to God for each person's blessings.

• Write "Thank you" notes to your support system expressing appreciation for their care and concern.

READING

Rejoice always, pray without ceasing, give thanks in all circumstances; for this is the will of God in Christ Jesus for you (1 Thessalonians 5:16-18).

RESPONSE

It is difficult to always be thankful, Lord. We cannot forget our loss. In spite of this, give us the grace to focus on your blessings, even if only for a while. Amen.

Holidays: Valentine's Day

Do you feel loved on Valentine's Day?

REFLECTION

Valentine's Day is an annual holiday which elicits a great deal of emotion both in the hearts of individuals and in the hearts of merchandisers. Valentine's Day has lost most of its spiritual meaning as the feast day of Saint Valentine and has become a predominately secular holiday. It is an important day for many because of the tradition to give greetings and gifts to loved ones. Millions of dollars are spent annually on candy, cards, flowers, presents, and restaurants. School children prepare cards for their parents and exchange cards with their friends. People of all ages love to be remembered on this day.

Many people react very negatively when they do not receive a gift—or at least a card—on Valentine's Day. Sometimes children are crushed when they are the only ones in their class to not receive a valentine. It is painful to be left out when "everyone" is sharing expressions of love. When a loved one has died, the pain is even greater. Unlike third grade when you didn't get a valentine and had the hope of receiving one the next year, you know that next year the pain will be there again. Instead of your heart being warmed, it is heavy and broken.

If your child was old enough to have made valentines in the past, you may have saved them. Looking them over on Valentine's Day can help to ease the pain as you remember the love with which they were given. Although it cannot erase the pain, it may make it easier to bear.

RITUAL

- Cut a heart from red construction paper and tear it in half. On one side list words associated with a "broken heart," such as death, impatience, and reminders. On the other half, record words connected with a "healing heart," such as conversation, friends, and time.

- Express emotions related to the death of your child by writing responses to a variety of "heart" related phrases, such as: cold-hearted, hard-hearted, heart-broken, heart-felt, heavy-hearted, and soft-hearted. Communicate the ideas in the form of a "Lune" poem. This pattern of creative writing is similar to a haiku, however, instead of counting syllables per line, words are tallied. The first line has three words, the second line has five words, and the third line has three words. For example:

  People may think
  That I am soft hearted
  If I cry.

- Make a Valentine for your child as an individual or a family project. It could be in the form of a card or a love letter as well as a poem or a picture. Display the Valentine in a prominent spot in the home or add it to a private collection of keepsakes.

- Place a picture of your child in a heart frame.

- If your child had a boyfriend, girlfriend, or spouse, remember your child's "sweetheart" in a special way on Valentine's Day and acknowledge the emptiness in her or his life as well as your own.

READING

See what love the Father has given us, that we should be called children of God; and that is what we are (1 John 3:1).

RESPONSE

Thank you, God, for the reality of love between parents and children. Thank you that it never ends. Although we may feel pain, help us to feel that love as well. Amen.

Hospitals/Medical Facilities

Are your thoughts of hospitals positive or negative?

REFLECTION

A hospital can be a beacon of hope for someone who is acutely ill. A medical facility can also be a reminder of pain, suffering, and separation for those who have lost a loved one. Unless your child died away from home or you have moved to another city, it is almost inevitable that you will have to go back to the hospital. You may become ill and need routine tests. Or, another family member or friend may become sick and be admitted as a patient. A return to the hospital may be anticipated with much dread. On the other hand, many people also remember very loving, helpful doctors, nurses, chaplains, and additional caregivers who helped to alleviate suffering and offered warmth and concern. One may associate both very negative and very positive thoughts with a hospital. They are seldom neutral. The sights, smells, sounds, and staff of the hospital bring back memories for most of us. Those recollections may be fleeting and partial—or we may relive the whole experience in our minds.

Even if one is able to avoid returning to the hospital, it is nearly impossible to avoid reminders of it.

Unless you live in a very large city, you will probably drive past the medical facility frequently. In our competitive society you will encounter advertising in the newspaper, as well as on billboards, radio, and TV. A day seldom goes by without some kind of a reminder.

It is easy to concentrate on the pain and suffering connected with a medical facility. It is somewhat difficult to focus on the positive at times. For many, the hospital is a place of healing. Perhaps we have those memories in our own past. We or another family member may have had a good hospital experience. We may have successfully recovered from an illness or surgery. We may have been ministered to by very caring nurses or technicians. Pausing to remember these things may help to overcome some of the painful thoughts.

RITUAL

- Donate items such as books, toys, or wall decorations to the children's area of a local hospital or regional medical facility.

- Deliver or send a gift of candy, food, or flowers to hospital personnel as a thank you for the ways in which they shared their "gifts" with your family.

- Offer talent and time as a hospital volunteer, possibly as a member of the auxiliary, a clerk in the gift shop, or a visitor to the patients.

- Organize a project for the pediatrics unit of a hospital. Decorate the space with children's artwork, coordinate regular visits from local entertainers such as puppeteers and storytellers, or prepare activity packets for patients to use during their stay.

- Say a prayer for patients and staff each time you pass a hospital or a medical facility.

READING

Do not worry about anything, but in everything by prayer and supplication with thanksgiving let your requests be made known to God. And the peace of God, which surpasses all understanding, will guard your hearts and your minds in Christ Jesus (Philippians 4:6-7).

RESPONSE

There are so many negative thoughts that can take control of us, Lord. Help us to center on what is good and pleasant. Above all, help us to focus on your love and care. Amen.

Location

Have you returned to the place of your child's death?

REFLECTION

When your child dies suddenly in a traumatic manner, the place where he or she died becomes very important to you. The news media frequently shows families gathering at or near the scene of a plane crash, a school fire, a train wreck, or a similar disaster. Sometimes it is in the hope that there is still someone alive, but usually it seems that there is a force drawing the families to that place—perhaps a desire to be close to their loved one for the last time. It makes little difference how far one must travel, we are drawn regardless of distance, expense, or time. Some may even experience dread in going to the place where their child died, but most of us do it, nevertheless. It may be our way of saying, "Goodbye, I love you."

When we arrive at the location of the tragedy shortly after it occurs we often seek out witnesses or first responders. We have a need to know what happened, not just from "official sources," but from people who were there. We may need to know the facts, but we also want to know that someone was present—or nearby—

when we could not be. While this may offer some consolation, it can also be comforting to remind ourselves that God was there. We may not have been able to hold our child's hand, but God held him or her in the palm of God's hand.

Some children die in a distant place that was important to them, like a young person killed in a mountain climbing accident in the Alps, or a diver killed in an underwater cave in the Caribbean. Your son or daughter may have pictures or mementos of that spot. You cannot help but be reminded of your child's life—and death—when you see them. Others die in a traffic accident or in some other circumstance close to home. It may be a location you pass every day. Although you may change your route to avoid seeing it, even picking another course reminds you of your loss. We can never completely avoid the reminders of our loss just as we can never avoid the reminders of our love for our child, as well as God's love for his children.

RITUAL

- Locate first responders or witnesses to the scene of your child's death and talk to them about the events surrounding the tragedy. Record the information in a journal or ask permission to tape their remarks.

- Obtain a copy of the accident report to read and review at the time of your child's death or at a time when you are ready to look at it.

- Photograph the location of your child's death or ask someone else to do it for you. Keep the pictures as a reminder of a place that might have been important to your daughter or son as well as a place that is now important to your family.

- Place a marker—such as a cross or a plaque—at the location of your child's death. Hold a memorial service or offer silent or spoken prayer at the site.

- Try to be present at the location of the accident that took the life of your child during recovery operations. Although it might be difficult to attend, it also offers the opportunity to ask questions, to talk to others who lost children in the tragedy, and to come to peace with the situation.

READING

> For I am convinced that neither death, nor life, nor angels, nor rulers, nor things present, nor things to come, nor powers, nor height, nor depth, nor anything else in all creation, will be able to separate us from the love of God in Christ Jesus our Lord (Romans 8:38-39).

RESPONSE

We thank you, Lord, that many of us can visit the place our child died and say, "Goodbye." Thank you for the knowledge that *name* is in your care. Amen.

Mealtime

Is there an empty place at mealtime?

REFLECTION

Mealtimes can be difficult for those who have lost a child, especially in families where meals are still social occasions in which the entire family is present. There are so many reminders of the loss—a vacant chair, an empty place at the table, the quietness that used to be filled with conversation or laughter, the jobs that an older—or even younger—child may have done, the favorite dishes that the child loved and the ones he or she disliked, and even the milk that doesn't get spilled anymore.

Meals are times when we are strongly reminded that the family is incomplete. Someone is missing. And he or she is missed. Some families may deal with this by changing patterns, for example, by eating out more often or by eating at a location other than the dining room table or the kitchen counter. Others may begin substituting different foods for the evening meal, hoping that the change may help them to not feel the emptiness of mealtimes. It is important to remind ourselves that, while we miss the child we lost, we can still cherish the family members we have. Meals can still be social events—even though they may be quite different from the events of the past.

RITUAL

- Create a montage of memories on a placemat to use in the center of the table on a regular basis or during special occasions.

- Invite singles, couples, or families to share a meal from time to time.

- Make an arrangement for the family table using a favorite cup, glass, or mug as a planter, or a special plate as the base of a floral arrangement.

- Plan to eat some meals in different locations, such as a gathering around the fireplace or a picnic in the backyard.

- Share family responsibilities by taking turns doing the jobs that were usually done by the child.

READING

When he was at the table with them, he took bread, blessed and broke it, and gave it to them (Luke 24:30).

RESPONSE

Be present with us, Lord, at our meal. Fill the emptiness of our hearts and lives. Nourish our spirits so we may serve you. Amen.

Media

How have you been affected by the media?

REFLECTION

For those of us who have lost a child from "natural causes," reminders from the media tend to be fairly simple. There is usually a death notice or obituary. Perhaps a family member or friend will take out an ad honoring our child. In most situations, there may be little negative emotion associated with the media.

When we lose a child in a sudden accident or under suspicious circumstances, however, the media can take on a completely different meaning. There may be a lot of coverage. We may find microphones shoved in our faces, newspaper photographers snapping pictures, TV cameras set up outside our house for hours on end, and radio reporters clamoring for a comment. It can be a terrible intrusion on our lives at the worst possible time. We can begin to feel like prisoners in our own home as we try to hide from the press, and we may be barraged by phone calls from reporters even in the sanctuary of our own space.

For some of us, the attention of the press may be experienced in a more constructive way. Some people may use the opportunity to pay tribute to a child who touched their lives in a positive way. We may turn on the TV to find a story about a sports team who retired a number in our son or daughter's honor. We may read about the efforts of neighbors to name a street or a park in memory of our child. Clippings or tapes from these reports may be treasured in the future as reminders of how our child brought joy and meaning to us, and to others.

RITUAL

- Be involved in writing the obituary for your child so that special and unique memories are included in this article.

- Save clippings about your child in a memory box or scrapbook.

- Set boundaries or limits in regard to contact with the media. If necessary, ask a family member, friend, or professional—such as a clergy-person—to serve as an intermediary between you and the press to establish appropriate contact and coverage.

- Take time—soon after the death of your child or many years later—to read or watch media accounts as a way of remembering how your child touched the lives of family, friends, and other people.

- Use church bulletins, club newsletters, and school newspapers as a way to communicate appreciation for the expressions of care and concern that were received after the death of your child.

READING

> But now thus says the Lord,
>
> he who created you, O Jacob,
>
> he who formed you, O Israel:
>
> do not fear, for I have redeemed you;
>
> I have called you by name, you are mine.
>
> When you pass through the waters, I will be with
>   you;
>
> and through the rivers, they shall not overwhelm you;
>
> when you walk through fire you shall not be burned,
>
> and the flame shall not consume you.
>
> For I am the Lord your God,
>
> the Holy One of Israel, your Savior.
>
> —Isaiah 43:1-3a

RESPONSE

Lord, whether the media is intrusive or respectful, we appreciate that our child is not forgotten. We thank you for his or her life and for the impact that he or she had on other people. Amen.

Memorials

Have you thought about a memorial?

REFLECTION

Memorials are a way to help people remember someone who has died, a way to insure that a person is not forgotten. Many families request that memorial gifts be made to charitable organizations in honor of their loved one. Some people donate vast sums of money to a university to have a building named for an individual. Others establish a scholarship or trust fund in memory of a daughter or son. Sports teams retire the numbers of special players. Veterans of foreign wars erect monuments; for example, Vietnam vets have their names engraved on a wall in Washington, D.C. Each of these memorials is a way of saying that someone was significant and should be remembered.

It is important to all of us that our loved ones are not forgotten. When we experience a loss, many times friends do not know what to do or to say. They may be afraid to even mention the name of our child for fear that it will cause us pain. A memorial is one way to say that it is all right to talk about him or her. In fact, it is a way to encourage everyone to remember—and to celebrate the time we shared together.

RITUAL

- Establish a memorial fund in honor of your child that will benefit a program or project related to church, community, or school.

- Get involved with the organization that receives a memorial gift, for example, serve as a speaker for a particular cause or assist as a volunteer on an occasional or regular basis.

- Hold a service of dedication for a tangible memorial (a model service can be found on page 186).

- Read Joshua 4:4-7 and remember that God told the Israelites to construct a memorial to help future generations remember what God had done for them. When the children asked, "What do these stones mean?" the Israelites were to tell them the stories of God's salvation.

- Since there are twelve months in a year (and since there were twelve tribes as well as twelve disciples), create a unique calendar—a rock collection—to record God's goodness to your child and to you. Select twelve stones and place them in a box or on a tray. Paint the rocks, if desired, and set them aside to dry. Think of ways that God is faithful and record the ideas on a piece of paper. God gives us life; God gives us caregivers and friends; God delivers us from difficult situations. Tie one thought to each month, if possible. The gift of life could be connected to a birthday or the theme of friends to a month with a special event. Using a permanent marker, letter the name of a month and depict one idea on each rock. All of the stones may be completed at this time, or one rock may be finished each month for a year.

• Start a scholarship fund and award a grant annually to a student with interests similar to those of your child.

READING

Then Joshua summoned the twelve men from the Israelites, whom he had appointed, one from each tribe. Joshua said to them, "Pass on before the ark of the Lord your God into the middle of the Jordan, and each of you take up a stone on his shoulder, one for each of the tribes of the Israelites, so that it may be a sign among you. When your children ask in time to come, 'What do those stones mean to you?' then you shall tell them that the waters of the Jordan were cut off in front of the ark of the covenant of the Lord. When it crossed over the Jordan, the waters of the Jordan were cut off. So these stones shall be to the Israelites a memorial forever" (Joshua 4:4-7).

RESPONSE

Lord, we pray that *name* may never be forgotten. May his or her life always be treasured not only by us, but also by our friends and acquaintances. Amen.

Movies, Music, Radio, Television

Is entertainment another reminder of your loss?

REFLECTION

Today's families spend a lot of time watching movies and television or listening to music and the radio. Some people have movies or music, as well as talk shows or TV, playing in the background all day. Many families watch television or videos every evening while others have a movie night on Friday or Saturday. Some children's lives seem to revolve around the latest CD or MP3 track. Often friendships, especially among teens, are defined by listening to music or by watching movies together. Many families have rules about who picks the music or the radio station in the car. In some families different people take turns selecting the music or station while in other households the parents or driver have the right to make the choice. All in all, forms of entertainment are a major part of our lives.

Because these things are so much a part of life, there are many ways that they may remind you of the child that died. The music—or noise—that began immediately when he or she came home from school is missing. Neighborhood friends and school classmates no longer spend time at your house. Collections of movies or music sit on the shelf. Fights in the car over who gets to choose the station come to an end. The television programs or movies you watch or go to see may suddenly be quite different. You might even notice an ad for a new movie or CD and your first thought may be how much your child would like it—only to be shaken back to reality seconds later. Every time you hear a certain song or see a reference to a particular movie you may be reminded of your daughter or son. When your child's favorite program—daily, weekly, or seasonal—comes on it may be too difficult to watch.

While it may not be possible to stop all the reminders that come to us every day, we can make choices that reduce them. It is important to remember that movies, music, radio, and television are not in charge of our lives. We are in charge of them. We can choose to listen or to watch—or not. We can change our listening and viewing habits. For many of us taking control of these things may be something we have been considering already.

RITUAL

- Change the station on the car radio or the music selection on the CD or tape player in the family vehicle, or spend travel time as an opportunity for silence and reflection.

- Hold a family meeting to decide whether or not to continue the "movie night" tradition. Make adjustments, as necessary, such as changing the day from Friday to Saturday or the location from home to a theater.

- Listen to music, read a psalm, or watch a video that shares a message of God's comfort and peace.

- Realize that the television will be on—at home and in other locations. Use these moments as an opportunity to remember the special times that you shared with your child.

- Sort through your child's collection of recordings. Keep those that have special significance and offer others to family members and friends.

READING

Blessed be the Lord,

for he has heard the sound of my pleadings.

The Lord is my strength and my shield;

in him my heart trusts;

so I am helped, and my heart exults,

and with my song I give thanks to him.

—Psalm 28:6-7

RESPONSE

Lord, there are so many reminders of our loss around us. Direct us and guide us so that we may make good choices for our own peace and for the welfare of others as well. Amen.

Moving

What if you move?

REFLECTION

Moving can be a very difficult experience at any time, but it is especially demanding for those who have recently lost a child. If the new home is some distance away, there is the loss of a support group like family, friends, and church. It might take some time to establish a support system in the new location. Fortunately, with telephone and e-mail, ties can usually be maintained with an existing group as well.

What makes moving especially difficult for some people is the loss of the "visual reminders" of a loved one, for example, the house and yard he or she played in, the school he or she attended. It is also a time when some must finally face the task of packing up the child's belongings and cleaning out his or her room. For those who have kept the room as a "shrine" to the child's memory, a move can be extraordinarily painful.

In our modern, mobile society, however, moving is a moment that parents who have lost a child often face. While moving requires us to leave many things behind, there are always things that we can take along. We usually can take not only memories, but tangible things as well, like pictures and possessions. Such things can help us to keep our "link" to the place we shared. It is also important to remember that we have a spiritual "link" that can never be broken.

RITUAL

- Compose an acrostic poem on the theme of moving. Print the letters of the word "HOME" vertically down the left side of a piece of paper. Use each letter as the beginning of a word associated with the theme. For example,

  Heart

  Occasions

  Memories

  Experiences

- Create a "blueprint" for moving from one stage of grief to another. Reflect on old doors to shut and new ones to open; consider windows to unlock to let in fresh air and windows to close to keep out chilling moments; remember times when the roof seemed to be caving in and others when it offered protection and security. Share the plan with a spouse or another family member.

- Reflect on the words of Psalm 139, especially verses 7-12. Remember that God is always faithful to us.

- Review Bible stories involving people who moved from one location to another. Old Testament accounts include Abraham (Genesis 12:1-4), Noah (Genesis

7:1), and Ruth (Ruth 1:15-19). New Testament narratives involve the disciples (Matthew 4:18-20), Joseph and Mary (Luke 2:1-5), and Paul (Acts 9:1-31). Read Jesus' promise in Matthew 28:20, "And remember, I am with you always, to the end of the age."

- Travel from room to room in the house and remember the events and experiences that occurred in each location. Offer a prayer in each place thanking God for the games played in the family room, the meals shared in the kitchen, and the rest received in the bedroom. Share memories with family and friends. In addition, take pictures to add to photo albums.

READING

By faith Abraham obeyed when he was called to set out for a place that he was to receive as an inheritance; and he set out, not knowing where he was going. By faith he stayed for a time in the land he had been promised, as in a foreign land, living in tents, as did Isaac and Jacob, who were heirs with him of the same promise. For he looked forward to the city that has foundations, whose architect and builder is God (Hebrews 11:8-10).

RESPONSE

Lord, it is difficult to say goodbye to a loved one. It is also difficult to say goodbye to the place we shared. Help us to remember that our connection through "things" is less important than the spiritual connection we have through you. Amen.

Name

What does your child's name mean?

REFLECTION

What's in a name? "A rose by any other name would smell as sweet," said Shakespeare. But, it is not quite that simple in reality. There are many aspects to a name. God's names suggest God's very being: All-Powerful, Always-Present, Ever-Faithful, and much more. God's names declare who God is and what God has done for us. People in Old Testament times were also given names that described certain attributes or characteristics. "Adam" means a man, or collectively, human beings. "Adam" is related to the word for ground or land, which according to the book of Genesis, connects to Adam's origin. "Sarah" suggests one who laughed. "David" means one who is beloved. In the New Testament, Mary was told to name her child "Jesus"—Savior—because he would save his people from their sins. Names, then and now, can be very meaningful.

Name associations do not end when your child dies. You are in a store and hear someone call the name of a child. You automatically stop and tune in before you realize that your child will not answer. There are many other triggers. You are on vacation and see a souvenir rack of bookmarks, pins, or signs with various names, including your child's. You pack your child's personal items and touch the backpack with his or her initials, the shirt with the embroidered pocket, or the visor with a favorite nickname. You visit with or talk about the beloved family member for whom your child was named. Or, the calendar reminds you of the "Saint's Day" related to the name you selected for your child— and the dreams and hopes associated with that choice. When any of these or similar events occur, memories and mental images of your child may come flooding back. This is a good time to remind yourself that Jesus, too, knows that name. Just as that name is important to us, it is important to Jesus, the Shepherd who knows each of his beloved sheep by name.

RITUAL

- In a prayer journal, use your most reverenced name for God and your own name—or your child's name—to write a prayer dialogue. Just as you would write a script, alternate between God's name and yours. Open yourself to a conversation with God. Begin with whatever is on your mind and heart, addressing God directly with the name you have chosen. Write what you feel inspired to enter as God's response to you, by name.

- Make or purchase a bracelet, key ring, necklace, or wallet card with your child's name on it and carry it with you, keep it in a special place, or wear it.

• Read or recite the words of Psalm 23. In this favorite and familiar passage, God is described as a shepherd. Throughout the Bible and in our everyday lives, God is experienced in many other ways—for example, as a friend, a guide, a healer. Alone, or with family members and friends, prepare a prayer illustrating additional metaphors to describe God. Complete the statement "The Lord is my . . ." with words such as comfort, helper, and hope. Repeat the phrases, one at a time, and follow each line with the response, "We praise your Holy Name." Conclude the experience by offering a prayer such as:

> Lord, God of all. You are many things to many people. Help us to spend our lives praising your Holy Name. Amen.

• Reflect on the meaning—or the significance—of your child's name. If needed, look up the source in a dictionary of names. Tell or write the story of how and why the name was chosen.

• Scripture lists many names for Jesus other than the name, "Savior," which the angel Gabriel instructed Mary to give to her child. Reflect on Jesus' names such as "Bread of Life" (John 6:35), "Light of the World" (John 8:12), and "The Way, the Truth, and the Life" (John 14:6). Some of Jesus' names describe special roles he fulfilled; others were given to help people understand him. Ask yourself how each of these names for Jesus represent your relationship with him. Use a different name for Jesus each day as you pray.

READING

Very truly, I tell you, anyone who does not enter the sheepfold by the gate but climbs in by another way is a thief and a bandit. The one who enters by the gate is the shepherd of the sheep. The gatekeeper opens the gate for him, and the sheep hear his voice. He calls his own sheep by name and leads them out. When he has brought out all his own, he goes ahead of them, and the sheep follow him because they know his voice (John 10:1-4).

RESPONSE

Thank you, Lord, for knowing each of our names. It means we and our children are important to you and loved by you. We know that you will never forget us—or our children. Amen.

Pets

What about a pet?

REFLECTION

At the moment of his master's death, Max the dog let out a piercing howl. His young owner had been several miles away in the hospital, but Max seemed to know what had happened. Max grieved for some time, but he was fortunate that someone could continue to care for him and provide him a home. Some of us are not able to keep a pet after its owner dies. We may not have time to care for a canary, a cat, a hamster, or a horse—or we might find that a "creature" is too painful a reminder of our loss. We have to find the pet another home.

In other cases the pet becomes a link to our loved one. What was important to him or her becomes important to us. What brought joy to our child brings joy to us. Or, like so many elements of grieving, we may discover that we alternate between finding pleasure and pain in being with and caring for a pet. In any event, we have choices to make. Most of us choose to keep the pet if we can, partly because we have become attached to it ourselves, and partly because it is a "part" of our child.

RITUAL

- Frame a photograph of your child and his or her pet and place it in a prominent place. Reflect on the special times they shared together.

- If another home must be found for a pet, take time to grieve this loss by holding a family farewell ritual.

- Read books, research information, take classes, or talk to experts about the best care for your child's pet.

- Remember that your child's pet has experienced a loss, too. Spend extra time with the animal or ask another family member or neighbor to help in this way.

- Use the routine of caring for an animal as an opportunity for meditation. While refilling the dog dish think about the caring qualities of your daughter or son or while chasing the guinea pig remember the persistence of your child.

READING

Look at the birds of the air; they neither sow nor reap nor gather into barns, and yet your heavenly Father feeds them. Are you not of more value than they? (Matthew 6:26).

RESPONSE

It's amazing, Lord, how important an animal can become to us. We know that you love all your creatures. Help us to do what is right for the creature(s) in our care. Amen.

$\mathcal{P}$ossessions

What about possessions?

REFLECTION

Many parents find their children's possessions to be a source of clutter and irritation. For many of us, the phrase, "clean up your room," is a constant refrain. Children seem to be accumulating "trash"—to the parent—or "treasure"—to the child—all the time. When you lose a child, all the "stuff" that was formerly junk may become valuable to you as well.

Some of what a child collects may literally be junk—items plucked from a trash heap with the hope of repairing them or recycling them for another project. Other possessions may have been acquired by trading something with someone else. Many things were probably purchased with allowance or hard-earned money in an attempt to develop or complete a collection or series. Most books, CDs, computer components, games, magazines, toys, and videos were likely given as gifts. Regardless of their source, these things may have been important to your child. They may represent a considerable investment of his or her time, imagination, and resources. In a very real sense they are a part of who he or she was—and is.

This can make decisions about what to keep, give, throw away, or sell very difficult. Getting rid of what was part of your child's life can be extremely hard to do. The process may be less painful if a sibling or best friend has similar interests and can put some of the possessions to good use. Sometimes parents may not be able to give anything away. It is important to note that we are all different in how we handle the situation. Neither keeping or disposing of your child's things is good or bad, right or wrong. What is important is that you do what is best for you and your family.

RITUAL

- Consider sharing your child's possessions with others as a matter of good stewardship. Many items might be used to help other children, youth, and adults. Think about offering books, computers, and games to families who might not be able to afford them. This type of giving should bring joy to you as well as to them.

- Find a place to display things that have special significance or pack unique items in a memory box.

- Photograph collections before giving them away or selling them and keep the pictures in a scrapbook.

- Spend one-on-one time with other children in the immediate and extended family, as well as classmates and friends, to sort through your child's possessions and to select items that they might appreciate.

- Use the items to teach other children hobbies and skills that your child enjoyed.

READING

Do not store up for yourselves treasures on earth, where moth and rust consume and where thieves break in and steal; but store up for yourselves treasures in heaven, where neither moth nor rust consumes and where thieves do not break in and steal. For where your treasure is, there your heart will be also (Matthew 6:19-21).

RESPONSE

Our treasure is in heaven, Lord, but things here are important to us too. *Name's* possessions remind us of who he or she was and is. Give us wisdom to know what to keep and what to give away. Amen.

Religious Items

Do religious items have special significance?

REFLECTION

Religious items encompass a wide variety of materials. A child may have a crucifix, rosary, Bible, medals, statues of saints, a picture of the Sacred Heart of Jesus, prayer cards, or scores of other things. Some of these objects may have very deep personal and significant meaning to a child. Items might have been gifts for a baptism, birthday, first communion, or holiday. One child who was afraid of the dark may have found great comfort in a crucifix because it represented to him or her the presence of the Lord. Another child may have found peace in saying the rosary in times of stress or illness.

In addition to these kinds of specific personal meanings, there are other meanings associated with religious objects. They point to realities beyond the commonplace things of this world, realities which are spiritual and eternal. They point to another realm where God dwells with his saints.

Because of these meanings, parents may feel very attached to the religious objects left behind by a child who has died. These things take on a new importance to the parents not only because of the memories associated with their child, but also because their child is now in the spiritual realm to which these objects point. They form a kind of physical connection to the spiritual world where their son or daughter now lives. What may have had special meaning to the child now may have very special significance to the parents.

RITUAL

- Add important religious items to a memory box or start a collection containing items that were precious to your child.

- Arrange your child's religious items in one central place in the home or display objects in several locations or rooms throughout the house.

- Carry your child's rosary, or another significant item, with you or keep it in your room.

- Offer some of the religious items to children, youth, and adults such as family members including siblings, aunts and uncles, cousins, and grandparents, as well as friends, pastors, and teachers.

- Pray near or with the items and reflect on the spiritual significance of life and death.

READING

The Lord is my shepherd, I shall not want.

He makes me lie down in green pastures;

he leads me beside still waters;

he restores my soul.

He leads me in right paths

for his name's sake.

Even though I walk through the darkest valley,

I fear no evil;

for you are with me;

your rod and your staff—

they comfort me.

You prepare a table before me

in the presence of my enemies;

you anoint my head with oil;

my cup overflows.

Surely goodness and mercy shall follow me

all the days of my life,

and I shall dwell in the house of the Lord

my whole life long.

—Psalm 23

RESPONSE

Lord, thank you for things that form a point of contact with *name*. We entrust him or her to your care, knowing that you love your children even more than any earthly mother or father can comprehend. Amen.

Restaurant

Was there a favorite restaurant?

REFLECTION

For some people eating at a restaurant is an everyday occurrence; for others it is an extraordinary occasion. Eating together—whether in the car at a drive-in in the neighborhood or around an elegant table at a formal function in another town—is one of the main ways we interact with each other. As a result, breakfast, lunch, and dinner are often problem times for people who have experienced the death of a child. Those who used to eat at home may go out more to avoid the empty spot at the table and the resulting emptiness inside. Those who ate out may eat at home or may try different restaurants in order to avoid reminders in familiar places. Some families may escape the pain of sitting down at the table by eating fast food on the run. Others may welcome a long, leisurely meal "out" to avert the "normal" routine. A restaurant can mean very different things to various individuals and groups.

"Breaking bread" together is an important social event. It is one of the rituals that binds us together as family, friends—and even as brothers and sisters in Christ. The travelers on the road to Emmaus recognized the risen Jesus in the breaking of bread. Jesus' disciples identified him in the sharing of a meal on the shore. Whether we partake of bread or fish, pizza or subs, eating together is a bond that ties us together. We may need to change our routine for some time in order to handle our grief, but we also need to consider the importance of sharing our meals together—wherever they are eaten.

RITUAL

- Look in a coupon book, newspaper, or phone book for new restaurants to explore. Print the name of each restaurant on a separate slip of paper. Place the pieces in a basket or box. When it is time for a breakfast, lunch, or dinner that will be eaten at a restaurant, select a piece of paper and try a new location for a change.

- Make a mobile depicting memories of your child's favorite restaurant. It might be a place where birthdays were celebrated or a location where "everyone" went after a school event. Cut a piece of construction paper or posterboard into a variety of shapes. Draw pictures or write words on each piece, including the name of the restaurant, favorite foods, menu items, special people, and memorable events. Punch a hole in the top of each shape and string a length of ribbon or yarn through the hole. Attach the pieces to a hanger or a hoop and display the mobile for others to see.

- Offer a prayer of thanks for the ways that God fills our emotional and spiritual hungers as well as our physical needs.

- Review biblical accounts involving Jesus' meals with other people. Include stories such as Matthew 26:26-28, the Last Supper; Luke 9:12-17, the feeding of the five thousand; and John 21:1-14, the breakfast on the shore. Reflect on ways that Jesus' presence is felt at mealtimes today.

- Share Remember When. . . . accounts of restaurant experiences by using a round robin method of story-telling. Invite each person to take a turn to add five words to the story. For example, the first person might say, "Remember when David fell asleep," the second speaker would continue, "before his third birthday cake," and the third individual could add, "was brought to the table." Continue until everyone has had a turn or until the story comes to a conclusion.

READING

As they came to the village to which they were going, he walked ahead as if he were going on. But they urged him strongly, saying, "Stay with us, because it is almost evening and the day is now nearly over." So he went in to stay with them. When he was at the table with them, he took bread, blessed and broke it, and gave it to them. Then their eyes were opened, and they recognized him; and he vanished from their sight. They said to each other, "Were not our hearts burning within us while he was talking to us on the road, while he was opening the scriptures to us?" That same hour they got up and returned to Jerusalem; and they found the eleven and their companions gathered together. They were saying, "The Lord has risen indeed, and he has appeared to

Simon!" Then they told what had happened on the road, and how he had been made known to them in the breaking of the bread (Luke 24:28-32).

RESPONSE

Thank you, God, that we have the freedom to change when, where, and how we eat if we need to. Help us to bind even closer to family and friends and to comfort and support one another. Amen.

Room

What memories are in a room?

REFLECTION

A child's room is his or her space—even if the room is shared with another family member or with a guest from time to time. A child's room becomes a reflection of a personality. It holds favorite clothes, collections, hobbies, sports equipment, toys, and so on. When the room belongs to a child who dies, parents may make a memorial out of it—or may at least have difficulty changing it for some time. A sibling who shared the room may have a fear of changing anything because making changes feels like disloyalty. Or, a sibling may change everything, acting in anger over the loss of a brother or sister.

Eventually most families make a change in the child's room. It may be given to another person or to another use. When this happens, the loss may be experienced again—this time with an added sense of finality. Repainting and redecorating, cleaning out clothes and other possessions, or even rearranging furniture may create a fear of losing memories of the loved one. Memories, however, can be evoked in many ways, not only from a space, but also from colors, objects, photographs, smells, and sounds. They are not dependent on a room, significant as that room may have been. What is important is the memory of the room—and keeping room in our lives for the loved one who has died.

RITUAL

- Compose a five-line diamond-shaped poem, a type of creative writing in which the theme is opposites or contrasts. The formula is:

    Line 1: One word which is an opposite of line five

    Line 2: Two words which describe line one

    Line 3: Three words which resolve the conflict

    Line 4: Two words which describe line five

    Line 5: One word which is an opposite of line one.

    Follow the formula and write a diamond-shaped poem to describe the process of re-purposing a child's room. For example:

    Empty

    Belongings removed

    Memories live forever

    Intangible treasures

    Full

- Go through every room of the house, including the child's bedroom, and re-dedicate their use to the glory of God.

- Leave a memory in the child's room when it is given to another person or another use. Memories could include the color of the paint, a picture on the wall, or a piece of bedding or furniture. Or, create a collage or montage, photo album, or video to retain a memory for the future.

- Read the children's book *Wilfrid Gordon McDonald Partridge* (Mem Fox, Author, and Julie Vivas, Illustrator. Brooklyn, NY: Kane/Miller Book Publishers, 1985.) Spend time in the room and reflect on the types of memories mentioned in the story— something as precious as gold, something that made you cry, something that made you laugh, something from long ago, something that makes you feel warm.

- Reflect on your child's new "room" in heaven. Find the word "heaven" in a Bible concordance and look up scripture passages such as Revelation 4–5 that describe it. Draw, imagine, talk, or write about this special place.

READING

Do not let your hearts be troubled. Believe in God, believe also in me. In my Father's house there are many dwelling places. If it were not so, would I have told you that I go to prepare a place for you? And if I go and prepare a place for you, I will come again and will take you to myself, so that where I am, there you may be also. And you know the way to the place where I am going (John 14:1-4).

RESPONSE

God, our child's room and possessions are some of those earthly treasures that we like to hold on to. Help us to remember that our treasure is, indeed, with you. All our lives are in your care. Help us remember that you will be with us always. Amen.

Seasons: Fall

How will you experience the changes of fall?

REFLECTION

Fall is a favorite season of many because of the beautiful colors of the trees, the exciting start of football games, or the rich variety of holidays. Fall is also a season of change. It is a time, especially in northern latitudes, when beauty changes to barrenness as leaves tumble from trees, temperatures begin to drop, and hours of daylight get shorter. The unpredictability of the weather seems to be accentuated as the variations become more extreme.

In many respects fall is like grief. When we lose someone important we feel barren and cold. The light disappears from our lives. We may experience sudden, unpredictable swings in moods, having a fairly good day one moment, only to plunge into despair the next. Even in our good times we anticipate that winter is coming. As bad as we may feel at a certain point, we know that it can get even worse.

It is good to remind ourselves that the seasons of the earth are given to us by God. The seasonal cycle that has been built into the creation serves a purpose. Without the seasons, the weather on this planet would be very different—perhaps so different that the earth would not support life as we know it. The seasonal cycles we experience, and sometimes dislike so intensely, help to produce the weather which sustains life. Often the difficult seasons of our lives, the experiences of change, help to support us as well.

RITUAL

- Consider the "coolness" of the fall air, and compare it to the times when you feel a "chill" because your child is missing—or because you are missing your child. Instances might include attending a football game, participating in holiday celebrations, or returning to school. Ask for God's presence in these "shivering" situations.

- Plant bulbs and wait for them to bloom in the spring.

- Celebrate the colors of fall—as well as the "colors" of your child's life—by creating a unique leaf design. Cut two large leaf shapes from waxed paper. Tear or cut small—approximately one inch—pieces of green, orange, red, and yellow tissue paper. Write a word or phrase to describe your child's "true colors," or personality, on each piece. For example, red—enthusiastic or spirited; yellow—radiant or sunny. Glue the tissues pieces onto one sheet of waxed paper in an overlapping design. Lay the other leaf on top. Using an iron set on warm, push it over the leaves to fuse the two pieces together with the tissue squares in between. Display the leaf in a window or store it in a memory box.

- Read children's books that explore the seasons of life, as well as the cycles of the spring, summer, fall, and winter, such as *The Fall of Freddie the Leaf* by Leo Buscaglia (Thorofare, NJ: Charles B. Slack, 1982), *To Everything* (San Francisco, CA: Chronicle Books, 1998), and *To Everything There Is a Season* by Leo and Diane Dillon (New York: The Blue Sky Press, 1998).

- Reflect on the spirituality of autumn. Even as nature seems to fall into a time of "death," the promise of another spring lies hidden in the earth. God, the Creator and Sustainer of the world, offers hope in every season of the year and in every season of our sorrow. Ponder the promise of eternal life evident in the seasons and write a haiku, a three-line Japanese mood poem, to express your thoughts. A haiku, which is unrhymed, contains seventeen syllables—five in line one, seven in line two, and five in line three. For example:

  Fall trees reflect change
  Vivid hues turn dark and drear
  God sustains all life.

READING

As long as the earth endures, seedtime and harvest, cold and heat; summer and winter, day and night, shall not cease (Genesis 8:22).

RESPONSE

We praise you, God, for the variety of the seasons. Help us to see the beauty of your sustaining presence around us. Amen.

Seasons: Spring

Can you celebrate spring's promise of new life?

REFLECTION

Spring is a time of rebirth and renewal. The sun begins to warm the earth and the coldness of winter starts to disappear. Green shoots break through the ground. Watered by showers, buds and flowers appear. Birds return from their winter homes. What looked dead becomes alive again. How appropriate that we celebrate Jesus' resurrection in the spring. Christ who was dead became alive again during the season in which all of nature is rejuvenated.

Just as spring brings us the promise of new life, Jesus' resurrection brings us the promise that death is not the end for those who believe in him. We may be separated by death for a time, but Christians can be assured that this is not the end of the matter. Jesus has conquered death and we share in his victory. Even in our grieving we can find comfort in knowing that our separation is only temporary. In fact we have God's word on it!

It may be difficult for many of us to rejoice in the changes we see around us in nature during the season of spring. Our grief may make those changes hard to appreciate. They can, however, be a reminder of the love of God and point us to his promise of life.

RITUAL

- Choose a bare branch and add "blossoms" to it to symbolize the "new life" associated with the season of spring. Cut or tear tissue paper into small squares. Crumple each piece into the shape of a bud or a small blossom and glue it to the branch. As each portion is added, offer a prayer of thanks for the new life God offers us through Jesus.

- Locate music for the hymn, "Great Is Thy Faithfulness." Read the words of the song, as well as the scripture passage on which it is based— Lamentations 3:21-24—as an affirmation of the way that God's love sustains and renews us every day.

- Purchase one or more packets of seeds and remember that seeds are a symbol of change, a sign of the promise of new life. The seed is the part of the plant that contains the life from which a new plant can grow. What appears to be dead has within it the promise of life. Use the seeds as a reminder of God's faithfulness during changing seasons, as well as God's steadfastness during the changing times of life. Consider going outside to plant seeds in the ground or start them in individual pots for use indoors.

- Reflect on the theme of "spring showers" and compare the gentle rains of this season to the tears shed as part of the process of grief. Cut or draw the outline of a rain/tear drop and write a shape poem around it. Ponder the process of growth and new life that results from both the rain drops and the tear drops.

- Take a nature walk and look for signs of new life, buds that are softening to form blossoms or shoots that are beginning to rise from old roots. Record the evidence of God's faithfulness in a journal or on film.

READING

But this I call to mind and therefore I have hope: The steadfast love of the Lord never ceases, his mercies never come to an end; they are new every morning; great is your faithfulness. "The Lord is my portion," says my soul, "therefore I will hope in him" (Lamentations 3:21-24).

RESPONSE

Lord, we see signs of life all around us. We find hope in them—and in your promise of eternal life to your children. Help us to focus on that promise and to anticipate its realization. Amen.

Seasons: Summer

Do you feel the warmth of God's love in summer?

REFLECTION

Summer is a special season, an opportunity for outdoor festivals, picnics, and sports. It is a time for beach parties, fireworks, and patriotic holidays. Summer is a period when people work in the yard together—cultivating gardens, planting flowers, mowing grass, pulling weeds, and watering lawns. Families spend time together on weekend or week-long vacations, and on leisurely summer evenings when children catch fireflies, play ball, and slurp Popsicles. Boys and girls are out of school, running through the neighborhood—and in and out of the back door. Summertime is a special season of family time.

Summer is also a season when reminders of the loss of your child are everywhere: the backyard or community pool, the bicycle or tricycle, the empty seat on the airplane or in the car on vacation; the list is endless. Each event has its own set of memories and its own emotions that those reminders elicit.

How a particular person reacts to these remembrances and emotions not only varies from individual to individual, but also depends on where a person is in the grieving process. One person may find it necessary to avoid many of the common reminders like the beach and the picnics. Other people may find it most helpful to jump right in again. Everyone is different. Sometimes, however, it is helpful to push oneself beyond what is comfortable. It is often by venturing outside our comfort zone that we begin to find a new level of contentment and peace.

RITUAL

- Choose a sunny day and take time to bask in the warmth of God's love. Find a park bench, a picnic table, or a sandy beach and spend time reflecting on the psalms, such as Psalm 23 or Psalm 148, that proclaim God's compassion as well as God's faithfulness. Arrive early to watch the sun rise or stay late to see it set. Take time to rest and recreate in the glow of God's love.

- Create sidewalk chalk drawings representing favorite activities during each season—that you have done with your child and that you will do without your child, for example taking a nature walk during spring, going to the beach in summer, playing in leaf piles during fall, and making snow angels in winter. Recognize that each season brings reminders of loss as well as opportunities for growth.

- Plant a flower, herb, or vegetable garden and compare the cycle of growth to the process of grieving that is occurring in your life. Try writing a "Tanka," a Japanese form of poetry that uses vivid images and literary devices such as metaphor, personification, and simile. Tanka poetry contains five lines and thirty-one syllables which follow the pattern 5, 7, 5, 7, 7 syllables. For example:

> Warm and waiting ground
> Embraces each tiny seed
> To nurture its growth
> God's encompassing Spirit
> Encourages me to risk.

- Read the book *Lifetimes: A Beautiful Way to Explain Death to a Child* by Mellonie Bryan and Robert Ingpen (Toronto: Bantam, 1983). It explores living and dying in caring, sensitive ways and explains the beginnings and endings of animals, plants, and people. The book emphasizes that all things have their own specific lifetimes.

- Volunteer to help at a summer camp or festival. Research groups that offer weekend or week-long opportunities for children with special needs, such as boys and girls suffering from an illness or those who have experienced a loss in their life. Support the program with a gift of money and/or time. Find out about community festivals which raise cash and comprehension for a particular cause and get involved in an event for an hour or a day.

READING

> To you I lift up my eyes,
>
> O you who are enthroned in the heavens!
>
> As the eyes of servants

look to the hand of their master,

as the eyes of a maid

to the hand of her mistress,

so our eyes look to the Lord our God,

until he has mercy upon us.

Have mercy upon us, O Lord, have mercy upon us,

for we have had more than enough of contempt.

Our soul has had more than its fill

of the scorn of those who are at ease,

of the contempt of the proud.

—Psalm 123

RESPONSE

Sometimes we find it difficult to participate in common experiences of life, God. We often find comfort in withdrawal. Give us the grace to find our comfort in you. Amen.

Seasons: Winter

Do you hibernate in winter?

REFLECTION

Winter can be a season of contrasts. We may experience the barrenness of leafless trees and the beauty of new-fallen snow. We may feel the chill of a cold arctic air mass or the warmth of a fireplace as we visit with members of the family. We may be enveloped by a long, dark night or be blinded by the sun shining on fields of white. We may experience the isolation of being "snowed in" or the warm fellowship of a Christmas party with good friends.

There can be other contrasts as well. Those who have lost loved ones may experience the warmth of family, yet feel empty and cold inside at the same time. We may be in a room full of people and feel lonely. We may be surrounded by others who are happy and cheerful, and we may even put on a smiley face, yet we may feel desolate inside.

Many people suffer from depression during the winter, especially during the holidays. Others experience it during the dark days of February due to the lack of sunlight in the northern hemisphere. It is easy during this season to contribute to our own depression by staying in and withdrawing. That may be what we feel like doing—and the weather certainly encourages us to act on that impulse. It is very important at these times to remind ourselves that spring is coming—and to look ahead to the new life that it brings. When we are grieving we need time to curl up and withdraw, but sometimes we also need to push ourselves to move ahead.

RITUAL

- Address the tendency to "hibernate" during the winter by making arrangements for a personal retreat or a silent day of reflection.

- Compare the "contrasts" of winter in the form of a "catalog" poem. This type of creative writing lists vivid descriptions of items related to a particular topic. For example:

Winter	*Winter*	*Winter*
Barren	Dangerous	Invigorating
Beautiful	Dark	Inviting
Bleak	Depressing	Involving
Bright	Dreary	

- Listen to music that expresses feelings, like the "blues," or play recordings that explore seasons such as "Turn, Turn, Turn" based on Ecclesiastes 3 or Vivaldi's *Four Seasons*, especially the "Winter" portion.

- Portray the "blues" associated with the season of winter, as well as the stages of grief, in the form of a painting. Express emotions by creating a picture with finger paints or water colors. Use cool colors, especially shades of blue, to reflect feelings at this time of your life and this time of the year.

- Share the warmth of winter by inviting others—family or friends, church members or classmates, social groups or support systems—to partake of a simple meal of hot soup and homemade bread.

READING

For everything there is a season, and a time for every matter under heaven:

a time to be born, and a time to die;

a time to plant, and a time to pluck up what is planted;

a time to kill, and a time to heal;

a time to break down, and a time to build up;

a time to weep, and a time to laugh;

a time to mourn, and a time to dance;

a time to throw away stones, and a time to gather stones together;

a time to embrace, and a time to refrain from embracing;

a time to seek, and a time to lose;

a time to keep, and a time to throw away;

a time to tear, and a time to sew;

a time to keep silence, and a time to speak;

a time to love, and a time to hate;

a time for war, and a time for peace.

—Ecclesiastes 3:1-8

RESPONSE

Lord, sometimes we need time alone. We also need to move ahead and affirm the life you have given us. Give us wisdom to know what we need to do today. Amen.

Sports

What about sports?

REFLECTION

For some of us, sports are a diversion. For others, they are a way of life. For many, sports define who they are. If we are fans of a team we may say, "I'm a Cubs fan," or "I'm a Notre Dame fan." If we play a sport we might say, "I'm a golfer" or "I'm a tennis player." Sports are extremely important in our lives. This may also be true of the child we lost. He or she may have been a fan, a player, or both. Sporting activities may have been a central part of life together as a family. When we lose a child, this aspect of our lives is forever changed.

If the family participated as spectators there is a change in family activities. Someone is now missing at games. Time together is different. Some family members may not even want to go to games any more. If the child was a participant, there are no longer games to attend—no banquets, meetings, or practices. The games may have been a social event for parents who befriended other players' parents. Now those contacts are lost or altered. Such connections may have been a large part of individual or family participation in church, community, or school social activities. Other children may have found friends there as well. These contacts may also be lost. Of course, if other children are still involved in playing sports, there may be plenty of opportunity for interaction.

Many children collect sports memorabilia. They may have their own trophies, souvenirs, game balls, uniforms, equipment, letters, and pictures. They may also have a collection of items from college or professional teams. You may have to decide as a family what to do with all this "stuff." That may be a very easy determination to make—or it may be very difficult. It is important to take into consideration the needs of all family members when making these decisions.

RITUAL

- Consider the needs and requests of children in the immediate and extended family, as well as those who may have played on a team with your child, when deciding what to do with sports-related items.

- Create a shelf or wall grouping of sports memorabilia your child collected or won.

- Give a gift to the team(s) on which your child played. It might be awards for a banquet, food for a celebration, money for equipment, or scholarships for new athletes.

- Invite someone to attend a sporting event with you, for example, other children in your son's or daughter's class or on his or her team, boys and girls in the neighborhood, or an older adult friend or neighbor.

- Stay involved with a sport or a sports team as a coach or a concession stand volunteer, or as a manager or mentor.

READING

You have turned my mourning into dancing;

you have taken off my sackcloth

and clothed me with joy,

so that my soul may praise you

and not be silent.

O Lord my God,

I will give thanks to you forever.

—Psalm 30:11-12

RESPONSE

So many things have changed, Lord. What was a source of joy can so quickly become a source of pain. Help us to find joy again in you and in your love. Amen.

Support Groups

Where do you find support?

REFLECTION

Support groups can be very helpful in the healing process. In support groups you have an opportunity to tell your "story" to people who are not only willing to listen, but who understand your feelings. In return, you listen to their stories and learn from their experiences. Without such a group it is easy to feel all alone—as if no one cares or understands. Finding out that you are not alone can be a liberating experience—as if a great weight has been lifted. And in a support group you may discover for the first time that people cope with grief in different ways at different times—the so-called "stages" of grief.

Support groups can be very beneficial, but they can have a "negative" side as well. While telling your story is helpful in the grieving process, it can be painful. You may even wonder if you want to go to another meeting. There may also be conflict between spouses who are at different stages of grief. One may want to attend the group and the other may not. He or she might even try to convince the other to stay home. It is important to invite the spouse who doesn't want to go, but not push or insist on a certain behavior. There may be other problems as well. Some support groups "fit" an individual and others do not. There may be personality conflicts between members, or one person may tend to dominate the group. Only you can decide if the group works for you. If you discover that you are in the wrong group, there is no shame in looking for a different one. Check with local agencies or the pastoral care department of a hospital for suggestions or for other possibilities.

RITUAL

- Check into options for support groups before you commit to attending one. Contact agencies like the American Cancer Society, institutions such as the pastoral care department of a hospital, and organizations including hospice for information and options. Research general grief support groups as well as those that are specific to the type of loss, such as miscarriage, stillbirth, or sudden infant death syndrome (SIDS), as well as groups that are geared to the age of the child or to the circumstances of the death. Talk with leaders, as well as participants, before you decide to attend a group.

- Consider the steps involved in finding support during the various stages of grief. For example, identify the first step that needs to be taken, decide on several small steps to explore, or contemplate a giant leap into a new experience. As an option, cut footprint shapes from paper and write one step on each sheet. Punch a hole at the left side of each shape and tie the loose pieces together to form a book.

- Journal the process that occurs before, during, and after attending a support group. Identify what was beneficial and what was not helpful. Resolve to grow from the positive, as well as the negative, experiences.

- Locate a set of blocks—any material and any size—and take time to identify your support system. Select a block and name someone or something that provides support in your time of sorrow. Include people such as family members, friends, coworkers, and counselors. Also identify strategies such as walking, storytelling, praying, and journaling. Of course, God might be at the base of the grouping—as the foundation—or at the top of the structure—as the summit of your strength. For a more permanent arrangement, write a name or a word on each block and glue the pieces together. If actual blocks are not available, draw or write the words on a piece of paper.

- Offer a prayer before, during, and after attending a support group. Ask God to be present with you, your spouse, other participants, as well as group leaders.

READING

So let us not grow weary in doing what is right, for we will reap at harvest time, if we do not give up. So then, whenever we have an opportunity, let us work for the good of all, and especially for those of the family of faith (Galatians 6:9, 10).

RESPONSE

It feels so good when people understand, Lord. Direct us to people who understand us and help us to be understanding and loving of them. Amen.

Vacations

Is vacation a time of re-creation?

REFLECTION

We all take vacations—a period of rest from study or work—in different ways. Some people get in the family car and go on an extended road trip. Other families spend their "free time" at the same lake or the same location, which may be just a few miles from home. Some travel by bus or train to distant cities or by air or ship to faraway countries. We all experience vacations somewhat differently. One thing that seems to be the same for parents who have lost a child, however, is that even as we move from place to place, our grief goes with us.

The usual seat in the car or the bed in the cottage may be empty. We might order one extra ticket at the amusement park, forgetting for a moment that there is someone missing. Our usual vacation ritual is unalterably changed. The vacation which was meant to be a time for refreshment and rejuvenation may become a time to be endured rather than enjoyed. We may have to "work" to find rest and relaxation. One goal of a "vacation"—a day or a week—may become "re-creation" as well as recreation.

RITUAL

- Consider the theme of "doors" while closing some and opening others on a vacation. For example, name familiar places you went to in the past and new spots you'd like to explore in the future. Discuss ways to help each other open doors to new opportunities.

- Create a sign post indicating directions your grief has taken in the past and the present as well as directions that it might need to take in the future.

- Look up the definition of the word "vacation"—a time away from study or work. Design a series of "mini-vacations"—ranging from one hour or one day to a few hours or a few days—that will offer a "time away" for re-creation emotionally, physically, and spiritually.

- Make a life map charting difficult or important events in your life; share with another how faith in God made a difference at critical moments.

- Reflect on the theme of "bridges" while crossing or viewing one or more of them on a vacation trip. A bridge may be a huge architectural structure that spans a major body of water or a modest board placed over a small stream. Regardless of its size, its function is to connect two areas and to enable people to get from one place to another. Talk about ways in which bridges are needed in families affected by the death of a child. There can be great distance between family members, extended family, and friends. Strained relationships may exist between children, parents, siblings, and spouses. Think of some of the bridges that are needed in these situations. Brainstorm words such as communication, honesty, imagination, knowledge, and support. Discuss ways to "build bridges."

READING

Come to me, all you that are weary and are carrying heavy burdens, and I will give you rest (Matthew 11:28).

RESPONSE

Vacations are supposed to be a time for re-creation. Help us, God, to re-create our lives and to find our rest in you. Amen.

Wedding

Do you wonder about a wedding?

REFLECTION

Weddings are the stuff that dreams are made of. Many little girls—and older ones as well—wonder who they will marry, what the ceremony will be like, where it will be held, what they will wear, and so on. Of course, boys have the same questions—spoken or unspoken. A wedding is an emotional focal point in our culture. It is also a great social occasion and an important religious event. It is one of the milestones of life that signifies leaving childhood behind and entering life as a productive, mature adult.

The wedding of one's child can produce many emotions in a parent. There may be happiness with the choice of a mate, pride in the beauty of the day, sadness that a child is leaving home, fulfillment that one has raised a child successfully, and so on. When one has lost a child, however, attending a wedding may produce many other emotions. There could be a feeling of being cheated out of family or grandchildren—or even the wedding itself. There may be envy that someone else is getting to see his or her child wed. These emotions may come not only while attending a wedding, but even when one hears about or receives an invitation to the wedding of the child of a church member, family friend or distant relative. Furthermore, there are the perpetual reminders of weddings—advertisements in magazines and newspapers, displays at bridal shows and shops, and even marriages on movie screens and television dramas.

Even the weddings of one's own children can bring up emotions that were long buried as we think about what might have been for the child that is gone. Fortunately, it is common to cry at a wedding. Others do not need to know if they are tears of sorrow or tears of joy.

RITUAL

- Acknowledge your deceased daughter or son at a family wedding through symbol at the ceremony, such as a rose on the altar, as well as words at the reception, like "*Name* would have loved to have been here. . . ."

- Feel free to decline invitations to marriage ceremonies until you feel comfortable attending wedding celebrations again.

- Give thoughtful gifts as wedding presents such as a Bible, a book of devotions, or a memory album.

- Read 1 Corinthians 13, a chapter often recited at weddings, and reflect on your love for your child, your child's love for you, and God's love for all of God's children.

- Spend time—silently, verbally, or in writing—reflecting on dreams, hopes, and plans that you may have had for your child's marriage.

READING

Love never ends. But as for prophecies, they will come to an end; as for tongues, they will cease; as for knowledge, it will come to an end. For we know only in part, and we prophesy only in part; but when the complete comes, the partial will come to an end. For now we see in a mirror, dimly, but then we will see face to face. Now I know only in part; then I will know fully, even as I have been fully known. And now faith, hope, and love abide, these three: and the greatest of these is love (1 Corinthians 13:8-10, 12, 13).

RESPONSE

Lord, we seem to miss so much when we lose a child. We miss *name*, but we also miss what might have been had he or she lived. Give us the grace to rejoice with others even as we grieve our own loss. Amen.

Resources

GATHERING MUSIC

GATHERING WORDS: Deuteronomy 6:4-9

HYMN: "I Love to Tell the Story"

LITANY OF DEDICATION

Leader: God began the story of faith, participates in its unfolding, and commands us to tell others of God's power and love. We can share God's story with the world in many ways.

All: The Bible tells of God's love through the ages by the power of the written word.

Leader: We can share God's message to the world through the arts.

All: The arts inspire us through the music we sing, the dramas we perform, and the pictures we paint.

Leader: Today we dedicate this memorial to God's glory and to the memory of *name*.

All: This memorial reminds us that God is present with us in our losses and that the ones we have lost are present now with God.

Leader: God commands that the story be shared and writes the story of his love on our hearts.

All: We are the story God is writing today.

Leader: May God grant us the courage to tell others how we have been blessed.

CLOSING PRAYER

Kum Ba Yah
We remember, Lord
the life and the gifts of *name*.
May this memorial,
which we now ask you to bless,
keep his or her presence alive in our memory,
and your love strong in our hearts.

HYMN: "Jesus Loves Me"

INDEX OF SCRIPTURE REFERENCES

Luke 2:8-11	Church Year: Christmas
Luke 24:28-32	Restaurant
Luke 24:30	Mealtime
John 9:5	Church Year: Advent
John 10:1-4	Name
John 11:25, 26	Church Year: Lent
John 14:1-4	Room
Romans 8:26, 27	Church Year: Pentecost
Romans 8:38, 39	Location
1 Corinthians 10:13	Classmates/Friends/ Teachers
1 Corinthians 10:31	Hobbies
1 Corinthians 13:8-10, 12, 13	Wedding
1 Corinthians 15:20-23	Church Year: Easter
1 Corinthians 15:42-44	Cemetery
2 Corinthians 9:7	Allowance
Galatians 6:9, 10	Support Groups
Ephesians 3:14-21	Holidays: Mother's Day and Father's Day
Philippians 4:6, 7	Hospitals/Medical Facilities
Colossians 3:12-14	Anniversary of Death
1 Thessalonians 5:9-11	Driver's License
1 Thessalonians 5:16-18	Holidays: Thanksgiving
1 Timothy 6:6-8	Clothes
Hebrews 4:14-16	Court/Trial
Hebrews 11:8-10	Moving
James 4:13-15	Dreams
1 John 3:1a	Holidays: Valentine's Day
Revelation 21:1-7	Family Picture/Portrait

GUIDE TO USING THIS BOOK

Phyllis and Ken Wezeman write about a parent's grief from both a professional and personal point of view. In their roles as pastoral minister and hospital chaplain they have consoled and counseled many who have suffered the loss of a child. And they too have experienced the death of children, in both their immediate and extended families.

Phyllis Vos Wezeman is a nationally recognized and widely published leader in the fields of religious education and faith formation. She currently serves as Director of Christian Nurture at the First Presbyterian Church of South Bend, Indiana. Kenneth R. Wezeman has been a pastor, counselor, and teacher and is presently Business Manager and Editor of Active Learning Associates. They are the parents of three adult children and grandparents of two grandchildren.